IS CHRIST DIVIDED?

IS CHRIST DIVIDED?

By

Elder Larry Young

© 2022 by Elder Larry Young

All rights reserved. This book or any portion thereof may not be reproduced or used in any manner whatsoever without the express written permission of the publisher except for the use of brief quotations in a book review.

ISBN: 9798849315683

SALUTATION

Praise the Lord and greetings in the name of our soon coming king, our Lord and Savior, Jesus Christ! To all my brothers and sisters in Christ, the blessed family of God who are destined for greatness in the Lord throughout eternity, which we will share with him if we love the Lord with all our heart, soul, mind, and spirit.

The body of Christ must be desperately determined to love one another, as Christ has taught us by his own earthly examples and holy lifestyle.

Please allow this book, *Is Christ Divided,* to nurture and bless your spirit and soul as you indulge into its pages.

Please pray and agree with me as I encourage the saints to love God and to witness to the glorious gospel of Jesus Christ every day of our lives as born-again Christians.

I strongly admonish each one of you to live saved, stay holy, and long for the coming of Jesus Christ, who will bring with him our eternal heavenly reward, which is a reward worth waiting for. God bless you and keep you, in Jesus's name!

TABLE OF CONTENTS

Preface		ix
Chapter 1	Who Died and Made You Judge?	1
Chapter 2	The Pharisees!	9
Chapter 3	Blessed Are the Peacemakers	19
Chapter 4	Send Barnabas	25
Chapter 5	Sanctified	35
Chapter 6	We Are All on The Same Team	41
Chapter 7	A Startling Observance	49
Chapter 8	It's the Principles That Matter	57
Chapter 9	God Is Sovereign	65
Chapter 10	Back to Eden	73
Summary		79
About the Author		83

PREFACE

The devil, the enemy, is very deceiving and full of tricks. He possesses many wiles (deceptive measures) to accomplish his mission, which is to steal, kill, and destroy. He comes to kill your faith, steal your joy, and destroy your hope in Christ. He wishes to keep the members of the body of Christ at each other's throats, thus weakening its power and influence on earth to win souls for the kingdom of God.

At times, he makes it difficult for himself to be noticed or exposed because he disguises himself as an angel of light (2 Cor.11:14) His ways are feigning and fake. He has mastered the art of deception. He's busy and truly on his job trying to wreak havoc and upset God's plan for unity among believers.

He knows that "if we are fussing and fighting among ourselves," then we have little or no time to focus on tearing his kingdom down. Petty feuding over mediocre differences will hinder our witnessing power and deplete our efforts to win lost souls. Therefore, he's compelled to do everything in his power to keep the members of the church at odds with each other.

There's so much division within the body of Christ. This group says that "we" are the only ones who are right. Another group believes that "they" have the only true revelation of the word of God. The Jews erroneously thought that they had a monopoly on God, believing that they were the only people of the

Almighty God, who, by the way, is no respecter of persons (Acts 10:34).

We cannot afford to be a divided church. The Lord stated that a house divided against itself cannot stand (Mark 3:22–25). It is a mandate that we combine our resources and forces to destroy the devil's evil influence in our world. Please remember, our strength is in numbers. A threefold cord is not easily broken, especially when the Lord is the third cord wrapped around the others.

There should be no schism in the body, which is separation and disruption (1 Cor. 12:25). The people of the world observe the division, fighting, and corruption within the body of Christ and are not fully convinced that we ourselves belong to Christ. Unity of believers will empower the church to carry out God's plan and divine mission to reach the lost. If we are to be successful in winning souls, then we must put away any signs of chaos, confusion, division, anger, and childish behavior.

Just one small spat of division can start an uncontrollable wildfire that's destined to destroy all in its path. Please consider, a little leaven will leaven the whole lump (1 Cor. 5:6). Don't become naive as to the destructive power of miniscule disagreements among believers. Most of our many so-called denominations were formed out of petty disagreements.

Not only will the devil use his demons to stir up trouble, but he will also use human beings to accomplish his will. As a talebearer stirs up a verbal blaze to an uproar by his cunning, clever, and deceitful words, so the devil uses troublemakers to cause division.

We must be aware and on guard to recognize the devil's tactics. Please be conscious of what he looks like, sounds like, and acts like. Don't be deceived by clever tricks and cunning behavioral stunts. Remember, Jesus said, you shall know them by their fruit. (Matthew 7:16, 20) If it looks like a duck, swims like a duck, and quacks like a duck, it's probably a duck! When at a railroad crossing of life, stop, look, listen!

The devil uses all these tools and tactics to separate, divide, and conquer the church of our Lord Jesus Christ:

Racism: (Acts 10)
Denominationalism: (1 Cor. 12)
Hatred: (Gal. 5:19)
Isolation: (Gal. 2:11–14)
Segregation: (John 4:1–9)
Separation: (Luke 9:49–50)
Division: (Heb. 6:1–6)
Non-affiliation: (Rom. 12:18)
Discrimination: (Acts 21:27–28)
Disassociation: (Rom. 14:1–10)
Non-communication: (Eph. 3:1–12)
Non-participation: (Eph. 2:14–16)
Non-reconciliation: (Eph. 4:4–13)
Non-consideration: (Gal. 6:1–5)
Non-appreciation: (Phil. 1:6, 8–21)

1 Corinthians 1:10–13 reads:

> Now I beseech you, brethren, by the name of our Lord Jesus Christ, that ye all speak the same thing, and that there be no division among you; but that ye be perfectly joined together in the same mind and in the same judgment. For it hath been declared unto me of you, my brethren, by them which are of the house of Chloe, that there are contentions among you. Now this I say, that every one of you saith, I am of Paul; and I am of Apollos; and I of Cephas; and I of Christ.

Is Christ divided?

A tree can be cut down much more easily if the axe head is

sharpened. Proverbs 27:17 reads, "Iron sharpens iron; therefore, a man sharpens the countenance of his friend." If we would unite, we could accomplish a lot for the kingdom of God simply by working together and not fighting against one another!

CHAPTER 1

WHO DIED AND MADE YOU JUDGE?

Why do we judge one another? Is it a genetic trait handed down from generations past? When we judge others, for whatever the reason, we behave as though we've done absolutely nothing wrong and have everything right within our own scope of life and relationship with the Lord. Judging others despicably takes the mantle of authority out of God's hands and seriously offends his sovereignty and supreme power to render righteous, fair, and true judgment.

I'm disappointed, troubled, and wounded when I am judged by others for whatever the reason. 1 Corinthians 4:3–5 reads:

> But with me it is a very small thing that I should be judged of you, or of man's judgment: yea, I judge not my own self. For I know nothing by myself; yet am I not hereby justified: but he that judges me is the Lord. Therefore, judge nothing before the time, until the Lord come, who both will bring to light the hidden things of darkness and will make manifest the counsels of the hearts: and then shall every man have praise of God.

In these previously stated verses, Paul tells the Corinthian church that their judging him will not destroy him. He further states that he does not even dare to judge himself, for he knows that God will judge him for all the deeds done in his mortal body. Romans 2:1–2 reads:

> Therefore, thou art inexcusable, O man, whosoever thou art that judges: for wherein thou judge another, thou condemn thyself; for thou that judges does the same things. But we are sure that the judgment of God is according to truth against them which commit such things.

Just know that God will faithfully render to every man according to his deeds. Paul is admonishing the church at Rome to judge nothing before the right time, and the right time is when the Lord comes again. Therefore, please don't judge and despise others for things you may interpret and deem immoral and unholy. God will disperse all unrighteousness.

Matthew 7:1–2 reads: "Judge not, that you be not judged. For with what judgment ye judge, ye shall be judged: and with what measure ye mete, it shall be measured to you again." Jesus tells us not to judge others, so that we won't be judged by him. Please consider that the same measure you use to judge someone else, God will use to judge you. He admonishes us also to not condemn, noting that when we condemn others, for whatever reason, God will condemn us by the very same motives and methods. God is Judge. He knows what our finite minds don't know.

Matthew 7:3–5 continues:

> Why do you behold the mote in your brother's eye, but won't consider the beam that's in yours? Or how will you say to your brother, let me pull the mote out of your eye, yet won't behold the beam that's in your own eye? You hypocrite, first cast the beam out of your own eye, then you shall see clearly to pull the mote out of your brother's.

Seriously consider this: Before we try to pull the splinter out of our friend's eye, let's strongly focus on pulling the plank out of our own eye. We've got so much to focus on in our own lives, we need not worry about certain things and situations in another person's life.

We are all the servants of the highest God. Who am I to judge another man's servant? There will come a day of judgment, but let's not worry about that day. Let us all pray to God that we do not possess a judgmental spirit. John 5:28–29 reads:

> Marvel not at this: for the hour is coming, in the which all that are in the graves shall hear his voice and shall come forth; they that have done good, unto the resurrection of life; and they that have done evil, unto the resurrection of damnation.

I really wonder how do we perceive others? Can we only see the specks in others' eyes while never seeing the trash in ours? Why can't we esteem or admire others with the spirit of grace by always showing mercy and compassion, without condemning them to doom and destruction? I'm quite sure that we have all sinned and come short of the glory of God and, apparently, have been proven by God to all be under sin (Rom. 11:32).

There's so much division in the body of Christ. One denomination is convinced that other denominations have obviously been deceived by the enemy into believing what they believe, even saying that they are praying that the other denominations can one day see the light and come to the truth. We spend too much of our free time arguing with others about who's right and who's wrong, when we should be complementing our similarities and the things that we agree on.

People who do not confess to be saved or claim to be a child of God can get along with one another much more easily than the so-called children of God. Those in the world, as we call them, are confused by what they see, hear, and observe. They see and hear certain denominations proclaim that they love the Lord, but on the other hand, they witness these same folks destroying and condemning other members of the body of Christ, all because (you guessed it) they're not with us.

Here's one of the most used statements by certain denominational groups: "You're not saved." And don't forget this one, "You're going to hell." Even their little ones have perfected this terminology down to a tee.

When I attended another church denomination, and I often visited many different members of the body of Christ, I was usually asked by the parishioners, "Why don't you come over and be with us?" They always seemed to allege that where I worshiped was not a legitimate place of worship and that God was not there with us. Truly amazing!

When they asked me to come over and be with them, I usually responded by saying, "I'm already with you." Then I would ask, "Do you love the Lord and walk upright? They would say, "Yes, we do." I'd respond, "then love God and your fellowman as yourself, and I'm with you, even though I'm on the other side of town or somewhere else." I still love the Lord and try to do my best to please him with a holy lifestyle and by loving all my brothers and sisters in the Lord.

Now when I visit other parts of the vineyard (other churches), I'm hardly asked that question anymore. When I visit other churches, I'm not concerned about what's over the door. I am more focused on what's in members' hearts. Jesus went everywhere sharing the gospel message without any reservations about categorizing people. He just went, determined to be a barrier-breaker and a light to a dying world.

Please consider this: If someone lives in a glass house, then I wouldn't advise him to throw stones at another's house. If you live in a glass house, it would be very beneficial to stop and think before throwing a stone at another's glass house, considering that the same person could pick up that same stone and chunk it back at your glass house. In other words, it would be very wise not to possess a holier-than-thou attitude. Isaiah 65:5 reads, "Which say, stand by thyself, come not near to me; for I am holier than thou." Deliver me from those who think that they are so much better than others, who act as though they have never done anything wrong before in their lives. Really!

In Mark 9:38–39, Jesus's disciples tell him that they saw someone casting out devils on the other side of town in his name and they forbade him because he was not with them. Jesus replied, "Forbid him not....For he that is not against us is on our part." What the Lord was trying to teach his followers was that they who love him are not against him but are on his side.

During the time of this scripture setting, James and John couldn't grasp the great miracle of a demon-possessed man having the demons cast out of him in the name of Jesus by the power of the Lord, because they were so obsessed with the fact that the man casting out the demons was not a part of their illustrious group. Jesus rebuked them, saying in essence: Leave him alone. A good thing has been done in my name; just focus on that above all else.

It really shouldn't matter who cast the demon out of an individual, or where it was cast out, or when it happened, just that the demon was cast out and someone got delivered from demonic possession. When the demons were cast out, God got the glory. For the sake of peace and the winning of souls, we shouldn't care: The end justifies the means if God gets the glory.

If we would stop fighting against one another and begin to work together as disciples and followers of the Lord, we could do greater works in winning souls for the kingdom. In working together, we could really accomplish a lot. Remember, there's great strength in numbers. Deuteronomy 32:30 tells us that if one can chase a thousand, then just two of us working together can put ten thousand to flight. Whether here or there, working together, the will of God is accomplished!

To expound a little more, I'm sure there are some that feel that they are too good to even set foot in another denomination's church because they (the so-called other folks) are not saved. I find it very peculiar that those same (too-gooders) want all those not-saved folks to patronize their businesses. They want you to come to their barber shop or beauty salon. They have no problem with you buying their barbecue plates and supporting their fund-raising events, proudly proclaiming "All are welcome."

Here's something to ponder: What if you were a business owner trying to get others to patronize your business? Would you say to them, "All sinners are welcome, come buy a barbeque sandwich or get your hair cut"? Once there, would you then proclaim, "I'll cut your hair, but you're going to hell"? How much business do you think you would have? Do you think that you would sell any of your products? I know that you wouldn't have many customers and wouldn't sell too many of your goods. Why? Because you used a despicable and deplorable method in trying to get others to buy your products.

Well, if you wouldn't dare display that type of behavior in selling barbeque, then why do you behave shamefully and disgracefully in trying to share the gospel message of Jesus Christ? Words and actions can easily wound and kill. They can be very destructive. Why not try grace and mercy, accompanied by love and kindness; with a little patience sprinkled on top? It works!

No one wants to be reminded by a sinful individual of the sin in their lives. Instead of talking about hell all the time, how about expounding on the eternal benefits of living a holy and saved life? Try showing them, by your own facial expressions, the joy and happiness of living for Jesus Christ. Be excited about the "better life" that you've experienced by accepting the Lord Jesus as your personal savior. Dwell on the great rewards awaiting the children of God.

Please don't throw away these straying, lost souls. Consider giving them the same chance and opportunity that the Lord has given you. Please extend mercy, tolerance, wisdom, and patience to hurting individuals. Give God a chance to change their lives for the better through his saving grace, which you have already experienced. For a change, let's do things God's way this time.

If you keep doing things your way, then your family members will dread seeing you coming to the annual family reunion with your nose stuck up in the air as though you are a professional sin detector who wants nothing to do with your loved ones until you need to borrow some money or need some other help from them.

I find the judgmentalist are notorious for barking out this phrase concerning others: "Ole Sinners." It appears these hypocrites are always playing God. Simply amazing! I thank God that I am not the judge of mankind. Please consider this: I don't know what one is saying to God at 3:00 a.m. in a prayer of repentance. Please ask God to deliver you from that "Ole Sinner" mentality.

I'm so glad that God will judge the world by that man, Jesus Christ. Some even have the audacity to justify judging others by saying the saints shall judge the world (1 Cor. 6: 2–3). Yes, the scriptures tell us that the saints shall even judge angels, but that judgment will take place only at its appointed time, which is during the Regeneration, when the Lord returns. I'll expound unto you, dear hearts, that we shall all stand before the judgment seat of Christ (Rom. 14:10). The Lord, and only the Lord, will determine where we will spend eternity. Thank God!

A portion of Psalms 75:7 reads, "But God is the judge." The Lord won't leave judgment to you, or to me, or to your bishop, or to my so-called denomination. If you are to judge, then please don't judge according to appearance, but judge according to righteous judgment. Don't be persuaded or convinced by outward appearances as to whether one is pleasing God or not. You've been drastically deceived if you think that God is going to leave it up to man as to where a person spends eternity!

Please note that if it's on the outside, it does not necessarily mean it's on the inside; however, if it's on the inside, it will show on the outside. Please, just live the life that God has set before you! Exhibit the glorious light of our Savior, while not exhibiting partiality to loved ones or fellow church members; for we are all a "work in progress" with a long way to go in perfecting ourselves before God and pleasing him.

The Word tells us that the father judges no man but leaves judgment to the son (John 5:22). The word of God will judge the works of mankind; it will determine your destiny of unspeakable joy or disastrous gloom. John 5:26–27 reads, "For as the father hath life in himself; so hath he given to the son to have life in himself; and hath given him authority to execute judgment also, because he is the son of man." The Son of God shall judge the deeds of all of mankind, he and he alone.

Yes, the saints shall judge the world. The truth of the matter is, we're judging them right now by our holy life before the Almighty God. The light in our lives exposes the darkness in the lives of others. Just live a righteous life and allow your holiness lifestyle to speak for a holy and righteous God.

I once read a billboard that said: "Be fishers of men. You catch them, Let God clean them."

Judge not that you be not judged; just be the light, that city on a hill!

CHAPTER 2

THE PHARISEES!

The Pharisees were members of an ancient Jewish religious party that carefully observed the written and moral traditions of the law of Moses. Their behavior, character, and principles were supposed to represent the true nature of the Mosaic law. (Were supposed to!)

They seemingly observed the letter of the law but not its religious beliefs. They considered themselves religious examples and the true and real demonstrations of God's laws. Their strict adherence of the law, according to their own private interpretation of it, clashed with the actual meanings and design of the Mosaic law. Their Pharisaical view of how the Jewish people should adhere to the law caused them to add several hundred other "man-made" laws and stipulations to God's ordained word given to Moses.

These additional laws placed additional heavy and cruel burdens on the people of God, not to mention the added stress that accompanied these vain and ridiculous commands. Their added laws were nearly impossible to observe and keep, and the Pharisees did absolutely nothing to lift some of these burdens.

By considering themselves as the only true masters and teachers of the law of Moses, they despised anyone who did not adhere to their strict interpretation of the law, considered them as disobedient to the Lord God, Jehovah, and as guilty of serious tribunal misconduct.

One of the many problems with their man-made laws was that they were not keeping them themselves. They were preaching and teaching one thing and living another; doing the very opposite of what they had demanded of the people. Sound familiar?

They defined the phrase "phony pretender" to the very letter, always finding fault in the actions of others while at the same time doing the very same things, if not worse. They were hypocrites, false-faced, fakers, not real, always pretending to be something that they were not. They were truly being very pious and virtuous on the outside without really being so on the inside. They were just acting the part.

During the time that Jesus lived on earth in Israel, the Pharisees had cornered the market as to who was the true established mouthpiece for God. These self-righteous zealots dared anyone to challenge their authority concerning interpreting and executing the commands of the law; after all, they were the noted Pharisees, the great religious leaders, the only elusive and extreme interpreters of the Mosaic law.

Jesus's holy life, the huge crowds that came to hear him preach, and his unique and anointed way of doing things posed a serious threat to the Pharisees' very existence and virtual authority in Israel. As far as they were concerned, he was attracting way too much attention to himself. In so many words, he was stealing their thunder, and this just could not be. Therefore, they felt it extremely necessary and urgent to put an end to his intense fame and popularity before either got out of control. They were so insanely delusional and intimidated by his popularity that they stated that the whole world had gone after him (John 13:19).

They desperately tried everything in their power to embarrass and humiliate him by assassinating his character every time they had the opportunity to do so. They repeatedly hurled insults at him, at times calling him a Samaritan, a lunatic, and an illegitimate child, being born of fornications (John 8:41, 48, 52).

Their attacks on our Lord showed the very nature of who they really were, constantly trying to trap him into saying the wrong things. Their determination to get him to say something against the law of Moses fueled them to go to greater lengths to use the Word to cause him to blaspheme. How extremely ridiculous and foolish it is for one to try to trap "the Word" with his own words. Truly unbelievable! Every time they would try to trap him in his words, he would counter by using their own words to convict them and expose them as to who they really were.

As God, robed in flesh, he had a way of silencing his critics with his words in such a way as to make them feel so guilty of the same sins that they were accusing others of and, eventually, coming to a point where they ceased to ask him any more questions concerning certain issues. God has such a profound way of confounding the wicked with their own words.

The final straw against Jesus was his announcement that he was Israel's long-awaited Messiah, which simply outraged the know-it-all Pharisees (John 10: 24–33). However, the very last straw of offense toward the Pharisees was when he openly and publicly called them that dreaded word, "hypocrite." The entire twenty-third chapter of Matthew depicts one of Jesus' last dramatic encounters with the Pharisees.

In Matthew chapter 23, these religious fanatics had had enough. Jesus had gone too far. He had done the unthinkable: humiliating them in the presence of all the Jews and their noted peers.

He really had to go now. They had to quickly come up with a devilish scheme to put him to death; after all, he was a blasphemer, claiming to be the Son of God. Something had to be done, and immediately.

The Pharisees—pretenders, the fakers, the self-righteous religious zealots—were always intimidated by the true righteous people of the world who will stand up to and against unrighteous actions displayed by phonies. True holiness will speak for itself. Don't be like the Pharisees (judge, jury, and executioner).

Apparently, Jesus must have truly exposed and mocked the Pharisees in Matthew chapter 23. He told the people that the Pharisees loved to sit in Moses's seat and desired all the important seats at the feast and that they loved to be called Rabbi and Master. They were truly caught up in titles and accolades.

"All they tell you," Jesus said, "that is what you do, but don't do like them, for they say one thing and do another." (Matthew 23:3) Many times, during this discourse, he angrily called them hypocrites. He said, "Woe unto you Scribes and Pharisees, Hypocrites; for you shut up the kingdom of heaven against men; for you neither enter in yourselves, nor allow those that are worthy to enter."

He told the gathered crowd of people that the Pharisees went to great lengths to make others like themselves, and when they were converted, they made them twice the sons of hell than themselves. He openly accused them of appearing holy and righteous on the outside, but full of filthiness, deception, and ungodliness within. He noted that they were like tombstones: beautiful on the outside but, inwardly, full of dead men's bones.

He reminded them that the Pharisees had a greater damnation awaiting them because they were always judging and condemning others (Mark 12:38–40). These Pharisees possessed a holier-than-thou attitude, always thinking that they were so much better than others. The prophet Isaiah reminded the Jews that their righteousness is but as filthy rags (Isaiah 64:6). Jesus' exposure of their hypocrisy was the ultimate insult to their integrity. Embarrassed and humiliated, they secretly plotted how they would put him to death (Mark 14:1–2, 10–11). It is amazing what envy and jealousy will cause one to do.

When these murderers brought Jesus before Pilate, this magistrate already knew that envy was the real reason behind them bringing him. He knew, without a doubt, that it was because of insane jealousy (Matt. 27:18). Oh, the deadly poison of jealousy and the lengths it will go to destroy anything that exposes it. Proverbs 14:30 reads, "A sound heart is the life of the flesh: but envy, the rottenness of the bones." Song of Solomon 8:6 reads, "Set me as a seal upon thine heart, as a seal upon thine arm: for love is strong as death; jealousy is cruel as the grave." The Pharisees would go to any lengths to destroy their opposition; even taking someone's life. They were the real wolves in sheep's clothing of the day, the real false prophets, the exposed hypocrites!

These Pharisees were a real act of complete deception and hypocrisy. On the night of Jesus' betrayal, arrest, and trial, the Sanhedrin (Jewish leadership) would not dare enter the judgment hall for fear that they might be defiled and would not be able to partake of the Passover feast. Here they were, falsely accusing a man of blasphemy so that they could have him put to death, but were worried about going into the judgment hall and being defiled (John 18:28).

They were worried about being defiled and not being allowed to partake of Passover, but had no problem killing an innocent man. Unbelievable. To some, certain acts are deplorable, while other, more disturbing and disgusting acts are understandable and rightly justified. Sounds like a hypocrite to me. I guess having a man killed because of their lies was not worthy of being considered evil, if they got rid of their hated enemy and dreaded adversary.

Going into the Roman judgment hall at Passover feast versus murder: which do you think was the weightier matter? I guess it depends on how one defines deplorable sin and its consequences. Sometimes we condemn others for the smallest of matters while excusing ourselves of greater sins, deeming them as justifiable mistakes to be overlooked.

To tell a little more, Jesus mentions one Pharisee's despicable prayer in the temple (Luke 18:10–14). Here we find a man bragging to God about how good and righteous he thought he really was. Jesus said that this Pharisee trusted in himself that he was righteous, and he sought to despise others. He even had the audacity to judge and condemn a publican there at the temple who also had come to pray. In gloating over his perfection and righteousness before God, he failed to realize that because he was a sinner, he too needed forgiveness and worthy of nothing but God's anger and wrath.

At the temple, the Pharisee stood and prayed, saying, "God, I thank you that I am not like other men are, who are extortioners, unjust, adulterers, and sinners, but a righteous man." He reminded God that he fasted twice a week and gave tithes of all that he had. He boasted and bragged about his righteous life. (He had probably been saved all his life.) I know that you've met someone like him somewhere on your Christian journey. I know you have!

Not only that, he refused to be thankful for God's mercy toward him, but rather focused his attention on another man's shortcomings. He did not realize that the same God who was aware of the publican's sins was not oblivious to his many sins as well.

In total contrast, the publican, in not going through the traditional rituals of religious rhetoric, humbled himself, admitting his sinful nature and asking God for forgiveness. Beholding his actions, the Lord said that this man, the publican, went down to his house justified, as opposed to this proud Pharisee who was condemned.

The repentant heart of the publican left the temple having his prayers heard. Forgiven and justified, he found just what he was looking for: God's grace and mercy. On the other hand, the prideful Pharisee left the presence of the Lord the same way that he came: condemned and guilty of judging others and lost. Troubling!

Jesus went on to say that those who exalt themselves shall be brought down and those that humble themselves shall be exalted. The way up is truly down. God deplores an arrogant and self-righteous spirit, and it will truly be rewarded with the punishment of eternal damnation.

Please stop walking with your nose all up in the air and acting like you smell stench in others, while it just might be your own smelly garments that are polluting the environment. Looking down on others and condemning them to hell won't work if you are trying to win lost souls to the Lord. Leave your judgmental spirit and your Bible at home when going out to witness to the world. If you want to witness, then witness first with your life. I would rather *see* a good sermon than *hear* one any day.

Jesus warned his disciples to beware of the doctrine of the Pharisees, which they believed was strict adherence to the law of Moses without any compromise. This so-called doctrine consisted of a very judgmental attitude, always laying their heavy burdens on the people to do things according to their imposed human-orchestrated interpretation.

The Lord further warned the disciples not to be entangled with the leaven of these hypocrites. Whatever the yeast is entangled with by association, it greatly influences. He was telling them to not get tied up with the ways and beliefs of these individuals, which would cause them to be guilty of practicing the same ungodly principles (Matt. 16:1–6, 11–12).

In their "self-righteous" attitude, the Pharisees were always finding fault in others, pointing fingers and condemning people for the very least of matters. Mark 7:2 reads, "and when they saw some of his disciples eat bread with defiled, that is to say, with unwashed, hands, they found fault!"

How quickly some tend to find fault in others. In John 8:1–11, the Pharisees brought a woman to Jesus whom they said was caught in adultery, even in the very act. They brought her to Jesus hoping to trap him in his own words and entice him to speak against the law of Moses. They said, "Moses in the law commanded us, that such should be stoned: but what sayeth thou?"

In accusing her of adultery, there was only one problem: Where was the man? She obviously could not have been caught in adultery all by herself. I ask again: Where was the man? You know it does take "two to tango." It's amazing how some can accuse another of a sinful act and, in the same breath, excuse or overlook the same sinful behavior in one's on self. Again, the man gets off "scot-free."

He went away unchecked, and without even a mere accusation, not even a slap on the hand. Wow!

So again, they asked what he thought about this situation. Jesus, being God, robed in human flesh and knowing all things, knew their motive behind bringing her and asking him this question. He simply responded by saying nothing at all. Stunned at his lack of reply and silence, they asked him again. Jesus, kneeling and writing on the ground, looked up at them and said, "He that is without sin among you, let him first cast a stone at her."

Being ashamed and convicted by their own sins and after considering his convicting words, one by one the Pharisees dropped their stones and slowly walked away. If you are guilty of even the least of sins, then drop your stones of judgment and destruction and walk away!

Isn't it amazing that the only one there who was truly justified to throw a stone at her because of his sinless life decided not to cast a stone at her? Instead of condemning her, he chose rather to have mercy and forgive her. He said to her, "Woman, where are your accusers? Does any man condemn you?" She answered, "No, Lord, there's none who condemns me." Then the Lord said, "Neither do I condemn you; go and sin no more."

Please notice that he did not condone her sins but neither did he condemn her, for he knew that there would be a day of reckoning and judgment coming. In mercy, he told her to go and sin no more. From my own perspective, I believe this woman lived the remainder of her life trying to please God, all because she had a close encounter with the grace of a loving, merciful, and forgiving Savior. Oh wonderful, merciful Savior, blessed redeemer and friend!

Remember, God's ways are not our ways. Isaiah 55:6–9 reads:

> Seek ye the Lord while he may be found, call ye upon him while he is near: Let the wicked forsake his way, and the unrighteous man his thoughts: and let him return to the

Lord, and he will have mercy upon him; and to our God, for he will abundantly pardon. For my thoughts are not your thoughts, neither are your ways my ways, saith the Lord. For as the heavens are higher than the earth, so are my ways higher than your ways, and my thoughts than your thoughts.

Those who have a legalistic attitude are in grave danger of hell's fires. Please note that he who keeps the whole law and yet offends at one point is guilty of all (James 2:10). The law was mainly given to show us our sins and many, many transgressions. It could not save us nor provide salvation's cleansing power.

The phrase "when they saw it" is commonly associated with the Pharisees. Luke 19:1–10 tells of a man, named Zacchaeus, who desired to see Jesus, climbing up into a sycamore tree hoping to speak with him. Jesus, seeing him in the tree, offered to go home with him to enjoy a meal. Oh, did I mention that Zacchaeus was a "publican," a dreaded tax collector whom the Jews hated? According to Luke 19:7, "when they saw it," they all murmured, saying that he was going to be the guest of a sinner. If you are notorious for calling someone a sinner, then you are probably (you guessed it) a Pharisee.

The law of Moses could not save us from our sins: if the law could save us, then there would have been no need for Christ to come and shed his precious innocent blood for all to have access to salvation's saving grace. The Pharisees notoriously judged others for failing to keep the law that they were not adhering to themselves. Please don't tell me to do right when you're not obeying the word of God yourself. Yes, I hear what you're saying. I hear your words, but I also see your actions, and your actions are speaking louder than your words.

Because of the grace and mercy of our Lord, salvation found its way to Zacchaeus's house. In addition, because of a close encounter with Jesus Christ, this sinful man's life changed for the better.

He repented, promised to restore everything he had deceitfully taken from others, and vowed to give a great portion of his riches to the poor. Most church folks would have no part of that type of fervent charity. A heart was transformed, and a soul was delivered, all because of love, mercy, and godly patience. The Zacchaeus's of the world just want to see Jesus, for they have heard that he is a friend of sinners.

The "when they saw it" phrase tells me that a lot of so-called religious folks spend their lives with their backs to the mirror. Positioned this way, they can see only the faults and shortcomings of others. However, if they really wanted to please God, they would flip the switch and live life facing the mirror.

Living every day facing the mirror would cause us to focus all day on our own lives, with little or no time to worry about someone else's shortcomings. I truly try to live every day with my face in the mirror, thus focusing my attention on myself. I've truly found that doing so causes me to judge my own actions and no other persons.

With my face in the mirror and not too close to the mirror, I can see every part of me. I can truly see all my faults and many flaws. If we want to please God with our lives, then let's live our lives in the mirror, always seeing and beholding "me." If we would judge ourselves, then we would have no time to judge others' actions and behaviors.

Jesus said in Matthew 5:20, "For I say unto you, that except your righteousness shall exceed the righteousness of the scribes and Pharisees, you shall not enter the Kingdom of Heaven." Please don't be an "accuser of the brethren" ([Jude 9] [Revelations 12:7–10]). Just live your life trying to please Almighty God. Be determined to abolish any judgmental terminology from your vocabulary. Please don't be a judgmental Pharisee!

CHAPTER 3

BLESSED ARE THE PEACEMAKERS

In the Lord's famous Sermon on the Mount, Jesus shared his views concerning the importance of a peaceful spirit. Matthew 5:9 reads, "Blessed are the peacemakers: for they shall be called the children of God." We are encouraged to follow the things that make for peace (Rom. 14:19).

The angels told the shepherds in Luke 2:10–14 that the Savior had come. Peace and goodwill were to be to all on the face of the earth. The Lord Jesus Christ will usher in the peace of God at his second coming and the earth will finally know the real everlasting peace of a loving God.

Let's strive, as the people of God, to follow peace with all men, along with holiness; for without peace and holiness, none will see the Lord (Heb. 12:14). The peace of God that passes all understanding will allow us to obtain a peaceful spirit and greatly influence our actions regarding conflicts that we may encounter as the children of God. It is very important, even imperative, that we possess this peaceful spirit, because it defines the nature of Christ. Remember, the Lord is not the author of confusion but of peace (1 Cor. 14:33).

On one occasion, two of the Lord's disciples were outraged about how the Samaritans were acting in refusing to accept the Lord as he journeyed to his destination with death in Jerusalem. They were so upset that they asked the Lord to call fire down from heaven and devour them as Elijah did in the Old Testament times.

Jesus sharply rebuked them and told them that they possessed the wrong type of spirit. He then stated that the Son of Man came to save men's lives and not to destroy them. He reminded them that it's not the will of God for his followers to use opportunities given by God to share the Gospel to, in turn, bash, discourage, and destroy others with harmful and hurtful words.

God is pleased when we exhibit pleasant and kind words to win the lost. Proverbs 16:24, 32 reads: "Pleasant words are as a honeycomb, sweet to the soul, and health to the bones. He that is slow to anger is better than the mighty; and he that rules his spirit, than he that takes a city."

Kind words are health to the soul and joy to the inner being. We should seek the wisdom of God in responding to certain behaviors displayed by others. It would be very helpful if we would ask God to closely guide our words and actions in order that we don't embarrass him and grieve the Holy Spirit. In Psalm 141:3, David said, "Set a watch, O Lord, before my mouth; keep the door of my lips." This was a profound, godly, and sincere request asked by the king.

Jesus said to his disciples in Luke 9, "You know not what spirit you are." I truly wonder at times whether we are aware of the damage we have caused by uttering cruel and hurtful words and phrases. A soft answer will always turn away wrath and douse the flames of anger and confusion. Wise and kind words create an atmosphere for God to work wonders in the lives of others.

Spiritual tolerance is a beneficial tool that can be used to win lost souls. Included in the fruit of the spirit is long-suffering (Gal. 5:22). Putting up with the shortcomings of others doesn't necessarily condone their actions, but rather allows God, through patience and righteousness observed in us, to transform them into the children of God.

None of us have gotten saved and pleased God with our walk before him overnight. It takes time for us to develop and conform to the ways and nature of Christ. Many trying and compelling years go into the making and molding of a child of God. Because God is patient with us and believes in our determination to surrender to his will, it causes us to acknowledge that we may fall at times yet knowing that the Lord hasn't given up on us. His divine mercy gives us an opportunity to restore our relationship with him.

We respond to his patience and mercy by not accepting a setback in our walk with him to deter our gradual spiritual makeover. What others can't see at first will be made manifest in the process of time through the glorious changing power of Almighty God. If we just give God a little time, he will save to the utmost our wayfaring friends and loved ones. If we would only exhibit a prayerful and holy life, then God will intervene, rendering his saving grace.

This generation could be the most challenging culture to win to the Lord in decades. They really have not known God's peace, a hope in Christ, or his real love. What they have encountered, tragically, is malice, bitterness, violence, disease, war, and hatred. Did I mention that, sadly, they have little or no knowledge of the God of heaven and earth?

Amos 8:11–12 reads:

Behold, the days come, saith the Lord God, that I will send a famine in the land, not a famine of bread, nor a thirst for water, but of hearing the words of the Lord: And they shall wander from sea to sea, and from the north even to the east; they shall run to and fro to seek the word of the Lord and shall not find it.

To be effective in winning souls today, we must possess a quiet, gentle, and very peaceful spirit. We must use every effort to douse the flames of hatred and violence and reverse the continuing downward spiral of a lack of knowledge of God and his word.

First, we must know Christ for ourselves. It is very hard and virtually impossible to tell the world about a God that we don't even know ourselves. How can we expound on the ways of God to others when we are not obeying his word and commandments ourselves? Anyone can talk a good game. God is looking for true worshippers, not phonies.

Be a true light of the God you profess to know and serve. Possess the spirit of the Lord and his righteous ways. Why are we so determined to constantly engage in confrontations about who's saved and who's lost? Being outraged about who's right and who's wrong has clearly taken away our genuine power to be effective witnesses.

We are commanded by our Lord and Savior Jesus Christ to be peacemakers and not hell raisers. Just be what the Lord has called you to be. Obey the great commission and go into all the world and make disciples!

Sadly, so many within the body of Christ have used the word of God to offend and destroy the lost, and that causes them to distance themselves from us and God's word. It's a trick of the enemy to try to get us to succumb to negative words and actions when witnessing to others. We know from God's word that offenses must come (Matt. 18:7), but let's not be guilty of being the offender.

As waters douse the flames of a burning fire, let's use the effectiveness of peaceful actions to douse the flames of division. It's so much more comforting to compliment the good things in one's life than to always bring out the negative things about another person. Why not tell them, Jesus loves you! It worked for the apostle Paul, and it will work for us today.

At the garden of Gethsemane, Peter pulled out his sword and cut off the ear of one of the soldiers that had come to arrest Jesus. The Lord immediately touched the man's ear and healed him.

Then he said to Peter, "Put away your sword, for he who lives by the sword will surely die by the sword" (Matt. 26:50–52). Violence always begets violence, but a peaceful spirit pleases God.

In our disagreements with others, we should try to come to a calm solution. Some simply need anger management. Violence, anger, hatred, and (God forbid) profanity should never describe the child of God at any time. Why can't we seek ways to get along? A quiet and peaceful spirit is always appropriate, for it gets God involved. Just try to get along. Ask yourself, is it really that serious that it causes me to argue and fuss with others? I mean, really!

The leadership of the church is commanded by God, through his holy word, to be not brawlers but peaceful soldiers on the battlefields of life. Titus 3:2 reads, "To speak evil of no man, to be no brawler, but gentle, shewing all meekness unto all men." Godly wisdom, accompanied by hospitality and fervent patience, fulfills the will of God in rendering services to a lost world.

The Proverbs writer tells us that the desire of a man is his kindness (Prov. 19:22). God uses his love and kindness, along with a gentle spirit, to save the world. When we move self out of the way and allow God's holy spirit to reign within, we truly allow God to be God, thus, showing the world who he really is. Some people will see God only in us and through us!

The world is in serious need of a sincere relationship with Jesus Christ. That relationship starts with the body of Christ. 1 Peter 4:17–18 reads:

> For the time is come that judgment must begin at the house of God: and if it first begins at us, what shall the end be of them that obey not the gospel of God? And if the righteous scarcely be saved, where shall the ungodly and the sinner appear?

Please greet one another with a word of peace. Jesus said on one occasion: "My peace I leave with you." Go out of your way to make friends, not enemies. Strive for a spirit of unity and togetherness every day. Find a mandate within yourselves to be an ambassador for peace. Be your own personal Nobel Peace Prize winner. Please greet others with the spirit of peace.

CHAPTER 4

SEND BARNABAS

There was a man in the Bible named Barnabas (Acts 4:36; 9:22–27; 11:19–24). He was a unique individual; a rare and very special person, one of a kind. He possessed an unbelievable character trait. He had the God-given ability to communicate and get along with others. He was a true friend to all who crossed his path. He probably never met a person in his daily life that he did not speak to. I truly believe that he greeted both friends and foes with a smile.

Denominational association, gender, or ethnic background never deterred him from associating with people. He loved people, regardless of race, color or creed. I envision that Barnabas believed that the only race that God was interested in was the human race.

Barnabas was given a nickname by the apostles that literally distinguished him from all others. He was called "Joses", meaning "son of consolation:" the one who could encourage others and virtually get along with all people. He viewed all, not by their differences, but rather by the fact that they were all God's creation. He would always give someone the benefit of the doubt, always seeing some good in everyone he met.

When the early church was afraid of the apostle Paul, formally,

Saul of Tarsus, it was Barnabas who brought Paul to them, persuading them that Paul was okay. Barnabas took the time to really get to know Paul. He put his own life and reputation in jeopardy because he saw something good in Paul and discerned that God had a great work for him. He assured the saints that Paul was no longer trying to destroy the Christian believers. He convinced them that Paul was now one of them.

God used Barnabas' gift of consolation to ignite Paul's missionary journeys. It was Barnabas who mentored this great apostle and evangelist during the early years of his ministry. We can credit Barnabas for introducing the grace of our Lord Jesus Christ to this former persecutor of the early church. It would be very rewarding and helpful to the work of the ministry if we would be like Barnabas and give others the benefit of the doubt. Please try to see people as the Lord sees them: merely candidates for salvation!

We cannot afford to be selective as to who we decide to witness to concerning the gospel of Jesus Christ, for all have a right to salvation, regardless of how vile and sinful their lives may have been. Titus 2:11 reads, "For the Grace of God that bringeth salvation hath appeared to all men." Just remember, the Lord shed his precious blood on Calvary's cross for all.

Sharing the gospel message shouldn't depend on how one looks or smells. Nor should social status, education, religious beliefs, or ethnic backgrounds disqualify a person from being introduced to the glorious saving power of Jesus Christ. Remember, no individual group has a monopoly on Almighty God. No people or nation can claim that they are the only ones that the Lord loves and cares about.

Sadly, some of the Orthodox Jewish nation believed that they were the only people of God. They had concluded that they were superior and, of course, all others were inferior to them. Acts 10:34 reads, "Then Peter opened his mouth, and said, of a truth I perceive that God is no respecter of persons."

Even though Jesus said that salvation is of the Jews, John 4:22, thankfully, it is not all about the Jews. Ephesians 1:3–7 reads:

> Blessed be the God and Father of our Lord Jesus Christ, who hath blessed us with all spiritual blessings in heavenly places in Christ: According as he has chosen us in him before the foundation of the world, that we should be holy and without blame before him in love: having predestined us unto the adoption of children by Jesus Christ to himself, according to the good pleasure of his will, to the praise of the glory of his grace, wherein he has made us accepted in the beloved. In whom we have redemption through his blood, the forgiveness of sins, according to the riches of his grace.

These Ephesians (Gentiles) were included in the "us" that the apostle referred to in this epistle, noting that before there was Jew or Gentile, the earth was inhabited by people created by God in his all-wise knowledge and providence.

I hate to burst your bubble, but there is no "us" or "them" within the body of Christ. One is either saved or lost, not in between. We are either on the Lord's side or on the devils. We're either on our way to heaven or bound for the lake of fire. Either we love the Lord, or we don't. We will either inherit eternal life or suffer eternal damnation. No, us and them among the saints. All that go to heaven will have been declared "us" and everyone cast to hell's flames will have been labeled "them." Period!

The Lord God determined and ordained who would share eternity with him before he created the world. All of mankind was created by God to praise and worship him. The Creator will tabernacle with his creation only according to his own discretion and purpose. Before we were identified as anything according to man's perspective, we were the children of God, molded into his own glorious image.

Jesus said in Matthew 11:28–30, "Come unto me, all you that labor and are heavy laden, and I will give you rest." The Lord is truly concerned about everyone's spiritual status. 1 Timothy 2:4 reads, "Who will have all men to be saved, and to come unto the knowledge of the God's truth". Barnabas understood this godly concept and strived to share the saving gospel of Jesus Christ with all he encountered daily.

The leaders of the early church, while stationed in Jerusalem, heard that the town of Antioch had received the word of the Lord. Because of extreme Judaism practices still harbored in some of them, they would not immediately go to Antioch themselves to inquire of the happenings there, but instead desired to send someone else there to represent them and the Lord.

They wondered just who they could send. Who would truly represent the Lord's grace and mercy to these proselytes? They needed someone with a spirit of compassion and of great patience; therefore, they chose Barnabas, the son of consolation.

Why Barnabas? What was so special about him? Acts 11:22–24 reads:

> Then tidings of these things came unto the ears of the church which was in Jerusalem: and they sent forth Barnabas, that he should go as far as Antioch. Who, when he came, and had seen the grace of God, was glad, and exhorted them all, that with purpose of heart they would cleave unto the Lord; for he was a good man, and full of the Holy Ghost and of faith: and many people were added unto the Lord.

The apostles heard that Antioch had received the word and they sent Barnabas to them because they knew Barnabas had the right spirit. They knew he could get along with others without much dispute. They realized that only Barnabas could accomplish the task of bringing Jews and Gentiles together in peace and unity in the name of the Lord.

The Bible tells us that when Barnabas arrived in Antioch and saw the grace of God upon them, he was glad and encouraged them to cleave to (get closer in their relationship) with the Lord. He did not attempt to skin a fish before he caught it. He was very happy that those of Antioch had made the first steps in walking with the Lord.

Verse 24 says that Barnabas was a good man and full of the Holy Ghost. He was endowed with the spirit of God and others testified that he was a good man. His holy life spoke for him and witnessed to others the glorious presence of God within him. Because of his unheard-of demeanor, many people were added to the church. When all else fails send Barnabas!

Grace works! The compassion of our Lord and Savior Jesus Christ will transform lives (Matt. 9:35–38).

As I close this section, I'm reminded of my childhood and the many life-changing events that come to memory. During my early years, I was literally surrounded by many pet dogs. They were of many breeds of animals, namely half-breed, and certainly not pure-bred animals. They were the typical street dogs (strays), but very lovable. These strays were commonly called "sooners": nothing to be proud of, and certainly nothing to be admired.

There was a unique character trait about these precious animals. They were very good dogs, even though they may not have been considered as such by some. Because of their humility, all the kids became very attached to an "ole sooner" dog.

Many of these dogs probably came into the neighborhood because they were abused by a previous owner. Some of these owners were so cruel and violent with their pets, physically and verbally lashing out at them on a regular basis. The abuse was so intense and increasingly violent until these precious animals simply left home and went across the street to be with other "sooners," where they were, at least, loved and cared for.

The former owners would come and try to retrieve them and take them back across the street. They would even try to persuade them into coming back by offering them Alpo, one of the best dog foods. The owners would graciously extend the food to them from across the street, but the sooner dog would not bulge, wagging his tail but refusing to go back across the street.

Yes, he wanted the Alpo, but he no longer wanted the abuse. He still remembered how hurtful it was when he was in the former owner's home. The food was great, but the abuse was devastating and very painful. If the owner attempted to cross the street to retrieve him, the dog would speedily run away.

Across the street, there was not much food to eat, and certainly no Alpo to chow on, but across the street, he found understanding, compassion, peace, friends, and love. He had absolutely no desire to go back to his former owner's house.

Today, people are leaving churches faster than rats leaving a sinking ship. Many big edifices are literally empty. Why is this the case? In most cases, leadership is so harsh, rude, and very hurtful to their congregations. The pastors spend most of their time bashing and destroying the fragile few that they do have in the congregation, not really realizing the tragic harm that they are doing to others and to themselves.

I've found that people are really hurting and confused in today's world. Not only do they come to church for correction, guidance and the word, but they also need exaltation, enlightenment, and encouragement. The church was designed by God to be a spiritual hospital to heal one's wounds, not to kill the wounded.

We as pastors need to understand that we cannot beat people into submission. People are not going to continue to come and pay their money for you to openly destroy them from the pulpit, always hinting and throwing out against them. Just keep on doing so, pastors, and you'll be preaching to the pews. Your congregation will do like the ole sooner dog and go across the street.

How is it that the apostle Paul, the former Saul of Tarsus, could do more in the evangelical field than all the other apostles put together? I believe he had a real understanding of the grace of God.

He simply shared the gospel message. For starters, he focused on getting close enough to people to get them to trust him before he continued to expound the word of God unto them more perfectly (Acts 18:26). He truly understood that he that wins souls must be wise.

We should ask the Lord to teach us what to say and what not to say, how to say it and how not to say it, and when to say it and when not to say it. It would be wise to ask the Lord to season our words with grace. The focus is not to allow the enemy to come in and then we get caught up in the flesh and offend our brothers and sisters with our words and approach, thus doing more harm than good.

In Acts chapter 8, Phillip went down to Samaria and preached Christ unto the Samaritans, and they received him. The Bible tells us that there was great joy in the city because of his preaching. Many souls were saved because a wise and tender-hearted man knew the powerful effectiveness of grace. Phillip gave them just what they needed, the gospel. He realized that they longed for an introduction to the death, burial, and resurrection of Jesus Christ.

Later, the spirit led Phillip into the desert to share the gospel message with just one man, an Ethiopian eunuch. Once again, wisdom and grace stepped in as Phillip approached this man's chariot, beholding him reading the scriptures. Philip kindly asked if the man understood what he was reading. The man replied, "How can I, except some man guide me?"

Phillip started right where the man was in scripture and expounded to him the word of God more perfectly. As they continued, the eunuch said to Phillip, "Here's water, what prevents me from being baptized?" They stopped the chariot, and the man was baptized. This man got saved and took the gospel back to his native land, all because a man well-versed in knowledge and the wisdom of our Lord and Savior Jesus Christ and the power of his resurrection shared a hope in Christ. Did I mention that his knowledge was accompanied by mercy and kindness?

There are a lot of Samaria's waiting to hear the gospel. They're waiting for you and me. Like Phillip, when we go, we must ask God to word our mouths to say the right things to win souls. Who will go to Samaria? Who will be like Phillip?

Just give them the gospel. Tell them that Jesus loves them. Stop looking at what they are, but rather what they can become. Please try to be a vessel that God can use to win lost souls. Be determined to move yourself out of the way and allow God to work his power and saving grace. Please consider your purpose and calling. Go into all the world and make disciples.

I often ask myself, what can I do or what do I need to say to win this person to Christ? I'm always asking God to give me the right words, the right actions, and the right response to be effective on the battlefield for the Lord.

In dealing with others, we should always be gentle and considerate of another's feelings. I'm reminded of a story I once heard of a farmer who went out one day to feed his cattle when he noticed that one of the young calves had, somehow, gotten an old rusty can stuck on his foot.

The farmer realized the immediate danger when he noticed the sharp rusty can was penetrating the calf's skin. What was he to do? If he rushed the calf, it would quickly run away, thus causing the can to cut deeper into the calf's foot and create a greater problem. He had to act quickly, but with wisdom and great caution, care, and gentleness.

So, he quickly went to the barn and gathered a bucket filled with corn. He then, very gently and quietly, approached the calf with intense patience. Because of his gentleness and prescribed caution, he was able to come close enough to the calf to secure it and then carefully remove the can from its foot.

The world is the calf with the destructive can called sin on its foot. The church is the farmer. In order to deliver them from the destruction of a sinful lifestyle, we must first get close enough to them to notice the problem and render relief. Kind and compassionate words will cause people to stop, look, and listen.

Think about this: If we are feeding hungry chickens their daily food, we cannot violently sling the food at them. Such cruel behavior will only harm the animals and cause them to run away. Then they will never get the nourishment they need and will eventually perish.

We have the food for the world, which is the word of God, but the world will never receive the word if we violently and angrily cast it at them. Remember, Jeremiah 31:3 reads, "The Lord hath appeared of old unto me saying, Yea, I have loved thee with an everlasting love: therefore, with loving kindness have I drawn thee."

If we would use the loving compassion of a caring savior, people's lives would change for the better and souls would be saved. A little tenderness accompanied by sincere kindness renders great rewards. The world is spiritually starving to death. Our former methods are obviously not working. How about changing our strategy and start trying things the Lord's way? I'm convinced; kindness works!

Remember, the harvest is white already! Just share the gospel message with grace and let God do the rest! When nothing else works, send Barnabas!

CHAPTER 5

SANCTIFIED

Sanctify/sanctified: *references:* John 10:36; 17:17–19, Joshua 3:5; 24:14–15,18–19; 1 Corinthians 1:2; Leviticus 11:44.

To sanctify or to be sanctified: to set apart as holy; being holy and dedicated; consecrated to a holy God; to consecrate and distinguish one's life; to be devoted entirely to God; to make holy; to declare sacred for religious use; spiritually pure.

Sanctify God: to revere and regard with deep respect; to honor, show obeisance to, and set apart from all other gods; to declare Jehovah as all mighty God of heaven and earth! ([Isa. 29:23], [Ezek. 36:23], [Num. 20:6–13]).

The "sanctified," the "special people," the "called out" ones, the "saints." These are the beloved of the Lord. This is you and me, the body of Christ: baptized, born-again believers whom the Lord deeply loves.

God chose the Jewish nation as a special people unto himself. Deuteronomy 7:6 reads, "For thou are a holy people unto the Lord thy God: The Lord thy God hath chosen thee to be a special people unto himself, above all people that are upon the face of the earth."

God did not choose them because he loved them above all other people on earth, but he desired to use them as examples to show the world how he wanted people to live holy lives. If he loved one nation of people more than all his entire creation, that would make him a respecter of persons, and that would make him sin ([James 2:1], [Rom. 2:11]).

God gave the Hebrew nation his written laws, the oracles of God, to first abide by themselves, and then to share, teach, and declare to all nations upon the face of the earth. They, themselves, failed God in doing so. Romans 3:1–2 reads: "What advantage then hath the Jew? or what profit is there of circumcision? Much every way: chiefly, because that unto them were committed the oracles of God."

We are all called to be sanctified. We dare not point fingers at others because of their sinful lifestyle, for such were some of us. At one time in our lives, we did not know the Lord in the pardoning of our sins, but now we are washed, we are sanctified, and we are justified in the name of our Lord Jesus and by the spirit of our God (1 Cor. 6:11).

As saints of the highest, we are a chosen generation, a royal priesthood, a holy nation, a peculiar people, that we should show forth the praises of him who has called us out of darkness into his marvelous light: sanctified by God's holy spirit! (1 Pet. 2:9).

We are set apart for his ordained purpose and chosen in him before the foundation of the world. He is depending on us to become what he has created us to be: called out, separate, holy, insulated but not isolated, saved and sanctified. (You get it!)

Jesus told his disciples in John 17:17 that he would sanctify himself that they might be sanctified. He was sharing with them that being sanctified only meant being set apart, holy and dedicated to God. (Saints!)

We are sanctified through the offering of his blood and by the Holy Spirit that dwells in us. Hebrews 10:10, 14 reads: "By the which will we are sanctified through the offering of the body of Jesus Christ once and for all. ... For by one offering he hath perfected forever them that are sanctified." A portion of Romans 15:16 reads "that the offering up of the Gentiles might be acceptable, being sanctified by the Holy Ghost." Have you received the Holy Ghost since you believe (Acts 19:1–7)?

The Nazarite was dedicated to the Lord. His life was to be lived in separation and consecrated to Almighty God. Hanna gave her son Samuel to the service of the Lord for his entire life. The Lord Jesus lived his life in dedication and submission to the will of his Father. His purpose was to fulfill his mission here on earth, which included portraying a holy and sanctified life for all to observe and duplicate.

He was, undeniably, the ultimate example of true holiness and godly sanctification. He literally set the bar as to how God wanted his creation to represent him. Yes, he was truly Emmanuel, which is interpreted to mean God with us (Matt. 1:23).

Please understand that it is virtually impossible for us to live a life equal to that of Jesus Christ, for he was truly God, robed in human flesh. But we should strive daily to please God in every aspect of our lives, going to extremes to be a light to a dying world.

Called out: The phrase tells us to come out from among them and be separate (2 Cor. 6:14–18). Be in the world, but not of the world; don't try to literally isolate yourself from others in having no dealings or communications with them, for that would mean that you would have to do the impossible and leave the earth: being isolated would indicate a judgmental spirit and thus, not be pleasing to God.

Just be who God has called you to be. In your life here on earth, put a difference between holy and unholy and between clean and unclean ([Leviticus 10:10], [11:44–45]). The Lord commands us to be holy, as he is holy. Some may say that no one is perfect. Well, the Lord is not asking us to be perfect: he is demanding that we be holy.

Please note, dear hearts that we are the light of the world. A city that's set on a hill cannot be hidden. Therefore, let's allow our light to shine so brightly in the world that everyone might see it and glorify our Father who is in heaven, for we are the salt of the earth and, as the people of God, we bring flavor to every place and people that our paths may cross (Matt. 5:13–16).

They were first called Christians, sanctified at Antioch (Acts 11:26). The citizens of this small town saw something in these believers that reminded them of the Lord. These new converts looked like, acted like, talked like, and behaved like their Lord. The people loudly declared, "These are Christians, they've been with Jesus."

Please don't be embarrassed or ashamed when someone calls you sanctified. If you are ashamed of the Lord before men, he will be ashamed of you before the Angels of his father. (Mark 8:38) It's really a cherished compliment; for those that are sanctified are chosen to be different and set apart for God's purpose. These are the true children of God. Sanctified: a blessed privilege!

I'm sanctified and not ashamed to be called as such. The song says, "When the saints go marching in, I want to be in that number; oh, when the saints go marching in." Be encouraged, for only the saints shall see the Lord Jesus in peace. The saints are those called out and chosen by God in Jesus Christ.

If the Lord didn't have a problem with being called sanctified, then why should we? John 17:17–19 reads: "Sanctify them through thy truth: thy word is truth. As thou hast sent me into the world, even so have I also sent them into the world. And for their sakes I sanctify myself, that they also might be sanctified through the truth."

Look up, oh you sanctified of the Lord, for your redemption draws nigh and closer than when we first believed. Yes, I'm sanctified and very proud of it. Oh, when the saints go marching into eternal life, this born-again believer will be in God's glorious, recorded number. Praise God!

The apostle Paul encouraged the Corinthian church to follow him as he followed Christ. He admonished them to live a life, as he did, that represented the Lord (1 Cor. 11:1). He was explaining to them that living for God was not an impossible task. He assured them that even though they were not perfect, they were redeemed! Wherefore, let the redeemed of the Lord say so!

My fellow Christian brothers and sisters, be encouraged, for God loves you. Please understand that sanctification and holiness is not a dress code, it's a lifestyle. It's not long dresses and cotton stockings in ninety-degree weather, nor is it pretending to be holy only on the outside and not living the same on the inside. Having a sign on one's back and proclaiming holiness does not make one holy. Being sanctified is simply being filled with the Holy Spirit and displaying a Christ-like demeanor for all to behold.

I truly wonder if others know that you are saved and sanctified without you telling them or wearing a sign on your back that says that you're saved. Can they just detect something different and unique about you? After Jesus' arrest, several men said to Peter, "You're a follower of Jesus; for your speech bewrays you." (Matthew 27:73) Oh, how I wish my lifestyle would not only tell people "Who" I am, but also "whose" I am. Thank God, my inheritance is among them who are sanctified (Acts 20:32).

CHAPTER 6

WE ARE ALL ON THE SAME TEAM

We've all heard the phrase "the body of Christ" (1 Cor. 12:27). I wonder if we take into consideration the real meaning of its concepts. The body of Christ (baptized, born-again believers) is one body with many members.

As our own human body is one body, yet it has many members, so is Christ's body. Within the human body, there are feet and hands, ears and eyes. It has a mouth and a nose, a heart and lungs, and so forth. Being many members with many diverse functions, yet all are the same body.

It's the same with the body of Christ. We, all by the same Spirit, are baptized into the same body. All members work together to keep the body functioning, healthy and alive. Whether we be Jew or Gentile, bond or free, we all are of Christ and in Christ (Col. 3:11). All of us are made to drink into one spirit. We cannot survive without one another, for we all need each other. Our mere existence depends on our working together as one body in Christ.

Wherefore, it's imperative that we all speak the same thing, and that same thing should be "Jesus is Lord." With unity in Christ, we are perfectly joined together with the same mind and judgment;

for how can two walk together except they agree (Amos 3:3)? We are truly in a carnal state of mind when we are determined to be separated and segregated from one another.

In our work for the Lord to win souls, our functions and purposes are all for the furtherance of the gospel. One plant and another waters, but it is our God who gives the increase. Therefore, he who plants, or he who waters is nothing, but it is God who gives the increase, for without God, we can do nothing. Remember, he that plants and he that waters are one in Christ. We are all laborers together with God (1 Cor. Chapter 3)

Here's my personal perspective of how all this foolishness of sinful division started. A mere parable of my own, not necessarily accurate or biblical, but just something to make you ponder a bit!

In the beginning of things in this country, there were two men who walked together in unison and agreement. Then one day Sam, as one is called, noticed that Dave, the other man, built a house slightly differently from the way he had built his house. Therefore, he was offended, because Dave's house seemed to look better than Sam's house. Did I mention that Sam might have possessed just a little jealousy because of the looks of Dave's house?

So, Sam decided to move away and distance himself from his brother, neighbor, and friend. He was determined to have nothing to do with his neighbor, all because of the difference in house blueprints. (Please stay with me.) Sam failed to realize that the difference in each man's design of houses should not have been a reason to separate and depart from one another. Mere petty differences seriously fractured a good relationship.

Sam decided to move into a neighborhood where other houses resembled his house and called that neighborhood the "cucumbers." All the cucumbers had the same type of house as Sam's. Unfortunately, one day one of the cucumber residents designed his yard differently from the other cucumbers and put a fence around his property, thus becoming slightly different.

Again, Sam was offended by his neighbor having his yard different from his and he decided to move again into another neighborhood called the "tomatoes." He finally was in a neighborhood that was in total agreement with him and what he liked, until another problem arose. One of his neighbors who enjoyed outdoor festivals pulled out a barbecue grill and began to barbecue.

Sam was outraged; he had seen enough. So finally, he decided to build an entirely new neighborhood of houses called the "potatoes" and drew up an outrageous set of rules and regulations that had to be strictly enforced in order to live in that prestigious neighborhood. Only potatoes were allowed in that neighborhood. Sam was finally truly happy. He was, at last, among his own kind.

Sadly, one day a horrific tornado ripped through the town and destroyed it, including the potato community. The destructive forces of the storm were unbelievable. Everything in its path was demolished. All the communities had suffered tremendous loss. Each community needed the others to survive and recover. They finally had to set aside their petty differences and work together to overcome this devastating occurrence. A powerful destructive storm bought enemies together to be friends again.

Sadly, today too many are seeking after their own kind. If one would just look around and take notice, they'll find that we are separated, segregated, isolated, nonaffiliated, disassociated and don't forget, hated; but we love God and are on our way to heaven. (Really!) We are on our way to heaven to be separated there as well. (Truly troubling.)

I'll have you know that if we can't get along here, then we won't be going there. There's no segregated heaven! I can't find it in the Bible. All of us who love God, walk upright, and keep his commandments are all going to the same place. One God, one heaven, one people. That's how God has it planned. It's God's way or the highway, and he doesn't care who has a problem with it.

I didn't make the rules and I'm glad I didn't make them. Being a man, I would be carnally minded. There are some people who I just wouldn't let into heaven. And on the other hand, there are some that I wouldn't keep out. In most cases, I wouldn't be fair. But God is fair and just. Do you all know that he is a righteous God, and he will do what's right? Thank God he's in charge.

Please allow God to be just who he is: God! He's got this! Believe me, he knows what he's doing. He's just too wise to make a mistake. Stay out of it. He really doesn't need our help. The last time I checked, God was still on the throne.

Paul had heard from others that there were contentions and divisions among the church which was at Corinth. Others testified that they witnessed envying, strife, and arguments among the new converts. One was declaring that he was a follower of Paul; another, a follower of Apollos; yet another, a follower of Cephas; and finally, others stated that they were only followers of Christ. This division had totally wrecked the church with havoc and had seriously put in jeopardy the ministry to win lost souls.

Paul had to quickly douse these flames of division that were sparked by Satan, the enemy of the church. He addressed the Corinthians with a question that caused them to reevaluate their relationship and callings in Jesus Christ. He simply asked them, "Is Christ divided"?

He reminded them that Apollos, Peter, and he, himself, were merely vessels used by God. Paul encouraged them to place the focus on the Lord and to give all homage and praise to Almighty God. We are all vessels, conduits that God uses to fulfill his purposes here on earth, and that purpose is to win souls for the kingdom of God. If we would take time to really examine (1 Cor. Chapter 12), we could find some startling concepts and facts about unity within the body of Christ.

The Bible states in Romans 2:11, "For there is no respect of persons with God." The Lord has no picks nor favorites within his church. All of us are loved and cared for by our God. He is truly concerned about all our well beings.

Too many are consumed with the notion that we are the church of_____! Or even stating that we are the_____ church! The only true church! Here are some scriptures that represent the churches of_____! You fill in the blanks!

Here are Bible-based scriptures to confirm the unity of the church:

The church of God ([1 Cor. 1:2)], [Acts 20:28], [2 Cor. 1:1], [1 Cor. 11:22]).
The church of the living God (1 Tim. 3:15).
The church of the first born (Heb. 12:23).
The angel of the church of Ephesus, Smyrna, Pergamos, Thyatira, Sardis, Philadelphia, Laodiceans (Rev. 2:3).
The churches of God (1 Cor. 11:16), (1 Thess. 2:14), (2 Thess. 1:4).
The churches of Christ (Rom. 16:16).
The churches of the Gentiles (Rom. 16:4).
The churches of Macedonia (2 Cor. 8:1).
The churches of Galatia (Gal. 1:2).

Just because we may do things a little differently than others do, does not give us the right to condemn and destroy each other. Please consider these truths:

There are differences of administration, same lord. Diversity of gifts: same spirit. Diversities of operations: same God.

For to one is given the word of knowledge; to another is given the gift of healing (but the same spirit).

To one, works of miracles; to another, gifts of prophecy.

To one, discerning of spirits; to another, diverse kinds of tongues.

To another, faith; to another, interpretation of tongues.

All the gifts, though diverse, are all the same spirit of God. God divides his gifts to everyone severally as he pleases, and all gifts are working together in that self-same spirit!

Christ loves the church (Eph. 5:25), the assembly of the called-out ones (Rom. 1:7). The church is indeed his body (Eph. 1:22–23). Wherefore, we the church should not forsake the assembling of ourselves together, as the customs are of some (Heb. 10:25), but we should come together in unity.

Being totally determined to come together in worship and praise, we should exhort one another by lifting one another through prayer and encouragement, knowing that the Lord's coming is rapidly approaching. It is extremely sad and disturbing that Sunday, our traditional day of assembly and corporate worship, is the most segregated day of the week for the body of Christ! (Awfully troubling!)

Jesus said about Peter, "Upon this rock I will build my church; and the gates of hell shall not prevail against it" (Matt. 16:18). Not Peter's church, nor Paul's church, nor your church, nor my church, but the Lord's church. (Some just don't get it!)

I would like to inform you that the church was founded by our Lord on the day of Pentecost, but it was ordained in the mind of God before the foundation of the world (Eph. 1:3–14). It was even mentioned before the coming of Christ. Acts 7:38 reads, "This is he, that was in the church in the wilderness with the angel which spoke to him in the mount Sina."

I really hate to burst your bubble, but you are not the only members of God's chosen body, the church. (Get over it: you'll be all right!) Profoundly, each individual group says that their doctrine is the only true way. My doctrine versus your doctrine! This is what we believe.

2 John 9–11 reads:

Whosoever transgresses, and abides not in the doctrine of Christ, hath not God. He that abides in the doctrine of Christ, he hath both the Father and the Son. If there come any unto you, and bring not this doctrine, receive him not into your house, neither bid him God speed: For he that bids him God speed is partaker of his evil deeds.

The doctrine of Jesus Christ is the doctrine of his Father (John 7:15–18). Some even define the Lord's doctrine as some new doctrine ([Mark 1:22–28], [Matt. 7:28–29]). Jesus always spoke as one with authority and that authority came from above.

People always seem to be concerned about what others believe and think about certain matters. What we really need to be focused on is what the Lord says concerning various issues (Matt. 5:21, 27, 31, 33, 38) I know words have been said of them of old to adhere to a certain way, but all that really matters is, what the Lord commands of his followers.

Here's something for our hearts to ponder: On a football team, all the players work together to get the victory. They work together because they are all on the same team. They've come to realize that working together as teammates gives them a good chance of winning the ballgame. The other team, all the fans, and all officials know that they are all on the same team because they all wear identical uniforms. These identical uniforms distinguish them from the other team. Our identical uniforms of holiness, righteousness, love, mercy, forgiveness, and truth tell the entire world that we are all on the same team!

The church, the body of Christ: that's all of us that believe in the saving grace of our Lord and Savior, Jesus Christ.

A friend of mine who happens to be of another race and another denomination (which has no variance on our relationship or our status in God, for we love God and our fellow man, and are striving to please the Lord with a holy life) told me that true unity of the body of Christ will not happen until it first happens in the pulpit.

Before the people of God can come together as one, it must start with leadership. The leaders must challenge themselves to step out of the box and step across racial and denominational lines and be willing to fellowship with each other for God's kingdom and the gospel's sake.

Do the unheard of and go visit another denomination's church, leaving your judgmental opinions back at your (only saved, only right) congregation and just see how others do things. Be determined to consider the plank in your own denomination's eye before trying to take the splinter out of another race's eye. (Oops, I mentioned "race"; sorry, forgive me!)

Please consider we all wear the same uniform, which is a holiness garment. We are the body of Christ, which is the Lord's bride. We are the baptized and born-again believers and are all on the same team.

I once was a member of a group of Christian believers of different denominational backgrounds, who met the first Tuesday of every month at a local motel for breakfast and to discuss scriptures and share testimonies. At the end of the hour-long gathering, we all would make prayer requests. My prayer requests would always be for the unity of the brethren. I think that God would be pleased if we would pray for unity of the body of Christ.

I heard a pastor once say that we may not be all under the same roof, but we should serve the same God and strive to please him with unity of believers in every aspect of our lives. As I stated earlier, we're all on the same team, and that team is God's team of righteous and victorious believers going unto all the world making disciples for the kingdom of God.

Please stop worrying about what they will think about you. Be concerned only about what the Almighty God thinks about you. After all, he, and only he alone, will determine who is welcomed to heaven and who is cast to hell. (Shocked??)

Our desire should be to please God ourselves and hear him say "Well done, my good and faithful servant." Why can't we get along? Why can't we love one another? For peace's sake and the saving of souls, why can't we agree to disagree? You strive to save souls in Ephesus, I'll strive to save souls in Thessalonica, and our friends will do the same in the uttermost parts of the earth; and at feast time, let all come together as one, okay?

Remember, we're all on the same team!

CHAPTER 7

A STARTLING OBSERVANCE

Blatant division and hypocrisy did not originate from the Lord. Jesus was the same everywhere he went. Here's a startling observation I've noticed when visiting some of my friends' places of worship. I've seen certain pastors of certain denominations and/or races not recognizing visiting ministers because of fear of offending their own parishioners. This is commonly called peer pressure. On one side of town, we're friends and brothers, but go across town and we segregate from one another and are strangers. Please don't allow peer pressure to cause you to miss heaven.

No wonder the children stare when we enter a certain edifice. You've put me under a segregated and separated magnifying glass. Your behavior towards me has made me feel unwelcome and very uncomfortable. I sincerely pray that the Lord will immediately rebuke me if I, at any time, engage in this type of disturbing and despicable manner and behavior.

I've found that some would rather disobey the commandments of God than offend the members of their own denominational group. It is sad to say, but some would rather die and go to a burning hell and be tormented forever than love all people and treat others with respect and equality, especially within the body of Christ. All who carry on in this manner should be totally exposed and declared to be in serious jeopardy of forfeiting eternal life. 1 John 3:14 reads, "We know that we have passed from death unto life, because we love the brethren."

Please consider this: If you hate me, then I'm not the one with the problem. It's the haters who hate, separate, and discriminate, and refuse to try to get along, who have the real problem. Those who practice this type of foolishness are compassed about with a deadly poison, but rest assured, hell's flames will take care of the problem. It will burn up the problem along with the ashes and shaft.

The saddest part of this kind of spirit of dissimulation (hypocrisy) is the children are watching. Hatred, division, and racism are not inherited; this behavior is taught. Just keep feeding a child a sour apple and, eventually, the child will become bitter. Just know that what is put into a computer is what will come out.

The children are watching and taking all this in. What message are we sending them? What character traits are we instilling in them? You could be the very one that determines whether your children, your sons and daughters, inherit eternal life with the Lord or are doomed to eternal damnation, which is separation from God forever. What you put into their spirit and mind determines their future.

Remember, a little leaven will surely leaven the whole lump. Just keep adding yeast to the flour and the dough will eventually rise. If the children keep beholding certain ungodly behavior patterns, they'll eventually pick them up and be converted to that foolishness. Please help them be like Christ. Give them a good example to imitate. Teach them how to love and respect others by your own holy and godly character and actions.

Galatians chapter 2 tells us that Apostle Paul went up to Jerusalem about fourteen years after his Christian conversion and took with him Barnabas and Titus, his son in the ministry. Titus, who was Greek, was not desirous to be circumcised according to Jewish customs and law. Paul also consented to him not being circumcised; for he was determined not to place any heavier burdens on him than were necessary according to the grace of Jesus Christ.

Paul constantly reminded the early church that a man was justified by the faith of Jesus Christ and by the Lord's holy spirit (1 Cor. 6:11). He let the Jewish followers of the Lord know that God had appointed him as the apostle to the Gentiles, as Peter was the apostle to the Jews ([Rom. 11:13], [Gal. 2:7]).

While Paul was there in Antioch, he noticed certain behavior by Peter and other disciples that troubled him. He observed that when the Jews were not around, Peter and certain others fellowshipped with the Gentiles, but when the other Jews returned, Peter withdrew himself from the Gentiles and gathered again with the Jews.

Paul, noticing this spirit of dissimulation practiced by Peter and others, confronted Peter to his face about this rather disturbing behavior, because he was to be blamed. He openly accused Peter of not walking according to the grace of Jesus Christ and not following the Lord's example. The Bible states that even Barnabas, the son of consolation, was caught up in this hypocrisy. Both Barnabas and Peter were behaving in this unusual way because of fear of what the Jews thought about them fellowshipping with non-Jews.

In Paul's sharp rebuke of them, he tells Peter, in so many words, "If you, being a righteous man, act like sinners, then how shall you persuade sinners to be like saints?" Talk is cheap. Almost anyone can say one thing, but living it is something else! Some are saying one thing with their mouths, but their behavior is totally different!

Just know that this type of ungodly character, left unchecked, will not inherit God's holy kingdom. As I earlier stated, separation, segregation, tribalism, division and such behaviors just won't be found in any parts of God's beautiful heaven.

The kingdom of heaven is so remarkable and very mysterious. Jesus on many occasions used parables to try to describe this unique environment and atmosphere. He would often say that the kingdom of heaven is likened to certain situations on earth to help us relate to and try to comprehend what heaven will really be like.

In Matthew 13:24–30, Jesus tells a parable of a farmer planting seed in his field. The Bible tells us that while the farmer slept, his enemy came and sowed tares (weeds) among the wheat, and then his enemy went on his way. After a while, the wheat began to sprout and come up out of the ground and, lo and behold, the weeds came up also with the wheat, thus causing chaos, troubles, and confusion in the field. When the servants saw what had happened, they were shocked at what they saw. They immediately went to the farmer and told him what they had observed. They said to him, "We know that we planted wheat, but where did these weeds come from?" The farmer calmly replied, "An enemy has done this."

The servants asked the farmer if he wanted them to pull the weeds out from among the wheat. He replied, "No, because while you're pulling up the weeds, you'll harmfully root up the wheat also, thus destroying the crop." He told them to just allow them to grow together in the field until harvest, and at the time of harvest, "I will tell the reapers to gather the weeds first and bind them in bundles and burn them, then gather the wheat into my barn."

To reflect for a moment, the Word tells us that, while he slept, his enemy came and sowed tares among the wheat. The enemy in this parable is, of course, the devil (Satan). The book of Revelation defines him as the great dragon (Rev. 12:9, 13:4). He is full of deception and tricks. He means no good to the people of the world and especially the children of God.

The enemy sows the weeds among the wheat because he wants to hurt the farmer by causing chaos and confusion. Notice the Bible says that while men slept, the enemy came. The devil came at night because he is the ruler of darkness (Eph. 6:12). There is no light nor righteousness in him, for he is full of darkness.

Division seekers are always wanting things their way. They have a perception of what's right and they are determined to make sure it stays that way. 2 Peter 1:20 reads, "Knowing this first, that no prophecy of the scripture is of any private interpretation." In other words, it's not about what you, me, or anyone else thinks about the matter, but rather what God says in his holy word. Division is like wildfire: it spreads very fast. It must be doused immediately before it does much harm and major damage.

Again, I reiterate, the devil sows the weeds among the wheat to cause trouble. He wanted to hurt this farmer by destroying his wheat crop. 1 Peter 5:8 tells us that the devil, our adversary, walks about as a roaring lion, seeking whom he may devour. He is desperately trying to embarrass and humiliate our God every opportunity he gets to do so.

He's always telling lies, for he's the father of lies and the truth is not in him (John 8:44). He's always stating untruths. Just ask Eve what it cost her, her husband, and mankind in listening to the disgraceful lies of this deceiver. He takes great pride in sowing discord among brethren, even going to great extremes to keep us warring against one another. Proverbs 6:16, 19 reads: "These six things doth the Lord hate: yea, seven are an abomination unto him. And one of those is a false witness who speaks lies, and sow discord among brethren."

Finally in the parable, the laborers asked the farmer if he wanted them to pull up the weeds from among the wheat. He said no, just let them grow together until harvest. We need to be in the world, but not of the world. We cannot isolate ourselves from the world, but we can insulate ourselves from the corruption of this evil world. If we try to take ourselves out of certain environments and circumstances, then how can we effectively witness to an ungodly world the life changing power of the gospel of Jesus Christ?

Let's identify the tares among the wheat and compassionately minister to them the word of God. One of the first things we could do is to tell them that Jesus loves them. We should continue to pray for them that they might receive the word of God and desire to give their lives to Christ, which is our main objective (winning souls). Please display the patience of our Lord. Remember, it takes time to exact real change. However, with God's help, all things are possible. Please be aware that this division is because an enemy has done this!

On one occasion when Jesus was addressing a large crowd, his mother and his brothers wanted to speak with him, but they could not because of the multitude of people surrounding him. So, they asked those closest to him to inform the Lord that his mother and brothers desired to speak with him. When his disciples told him, he responded by saying, "Who is my mother and who is my brother?" Immediately he stretched forth his hand toward his disciples and said, "Behold my mother and my brothers and my sisters, for whoever does the will of my father, the same is my mother, my brother, and my sister." Whoever does God's will shall be the children of God!

When certain ones ask me to tell them what denomination I belong to, I usually shock them with my response. I tell them that I'm determined to be just what God has called me to be. Leviticus 11:44 reads, "For I am the Lord your God: ye shall therefore sanctify yourselves, and ye shall be holy; for I am holy." I'm only what God has called me to be (holy), which means striving daily to be more like Jesus Christ. That's all I am, holy. We should always strive to be more like our God. Be holy, not denominational.

One thing I will say is: I am persuaded, without controversy, that great is the mystery of godliness; for God was manifest in the flesh, justified in the spirit, seen of angels, preached unto the Gentiles, believed on in the world, received up into glory (1 Tim. 3:16). You can be whatever you choose to be. I've decided to be holy. I'm not going to allow a denominational tag to prevent me from fellowshipping with my brothers and sisters. Be ye holy!

As I said earlier, some say no one is perfect. Well, God is not asking you to be perfect, he's demanding that you be holy. Be followers of Christ as the holy people of God. The priests, pastors, and prophets are commanded and encouraged to teach the people how to live holy (Eze. 44:21–24). The people are to be taught how to live a holy life before God. Oh, men and women of God, be holy. Always represent God. Be holy, for God has not called us unto uncleanness, but unto holiness (1 Thess. 4:7).

Paul writes in 1 Thessalonians 3:12–13:

> The Lord makes you to increase and abound in love toward another, and toward all men, even as we do toward you: To the end he may [e]stablish your hearts unblameable in holiness before God, even our Father, at the coming of our Lord Jesus Christ with all his saints.

The twain has to be one. In fact, it must be one! We're all in this together. God has one plan: that all men be saved and come into the knowledge of Jesus Christ. The enemy hates our Lord and Savior, Jesus Christ, and he desires to destroy all his followers (the saints). The devil sows division within the body of Christ. His battery arsenal is composed of the many scattering tactics of lies, cunning devices, conniving tricks, and all other means that he can use.

He is desperately trying to spiritually annihilate the church. He's always stirring up trouble, for he is the master of deception. If he can keep us at each other's throats while prompting us to argue and fight among ourselves, then he can gain a strong hold and advantage over us. 1 Corinthians 14:33 reads, "For God is not the author of confusion, but of peace, as in all churches of the saints."

We must stay focused. We must work together as the Lord's ambassadors (2 Cor. 5:20). We must be determined to always display the love and character of Jesus Christ; for we are one army of spiritual soldiers fighting together to defend the kingdom of God and to protect our precious souls from destruction. Remember, we're all in this together: your enemy is my enemy; your God is my God. The twain must be one.

Let's love with fervent charity, for charity shall cover a multitude of faults (1 Pet. 4:8). Let's try to look past other misfortunes and noticeable sins and forgive one another while loving each other as Christ has commanded us in his word. John 13:34–35 reads, "A new commandment I give you, that you love one another; as I have loved you, that ye also love one another. By this shall all men know that ye are my disciples, if ye have love one to another."

For those of you who desire to play the "race" card, I'll have you know that it's not about black and white, but rather what's right. Just think about it: we all come from Adam. We all come from the dust of the earth, and when we die, our sinful flesh will return to the earth. Ecclesiastes 12:7 reads, "Then shall the dust return to the earth as it was: and the spirit return unto God who gave it."

1 John 3:2 reads, "Beloved, now are we the sons of God, and it doth not yet appear what we shall be: but we know that, when he shall appear, we shall be like him; for we shall see him as he is." We don't even know what we shall be in the end, but we do know that we shall be like Christ. For all of us, when cut, bleed red blood! (Selah.)

A judgmental and condemning spirit will not render peace and happiness but, rather, a bitter and discouraging attitude that others will observe. Jesus is the reason the sun shines all around me. His radiance of peaceful joy causes me to proclaim to the whole world, through my facial expressions, that our God is good, and I am so blessed and privileged just to know him. Smile, hold your head up; be happy; be glad. Greet others with kindness and a word of peace. Oh, the glorious joy that salvation brings to the child of God. Just a startling observance.

CHAPTER 8

IT'S THE PRINCIPLES THAT MATTER

Do you ever wonder what pleases God? What impresses the Almighty? What does the Lord require of us? In a world of people seeking to impress each other, we, as children of God, should strive to live our lives determined to please God by the way we treat others.

Micah 6:7–8 reads:

> Will the Lord be pleased with thousands of rams, or with ten thousands of rivers of oil? Shall I give my firstborn for my transgression, the fruit of my body for the sin of my soul? He hath shewed thee, O man, what is good; and what does the Lord require of thee, but to do justly, to love mercy, and to walk humbly with your God?

God is impressed when we do right, show mercy to others, and possess a humble spirit. He is pleased when we display a prayerful life, a compassionate heart, a kind demeanor, an excellent spirit, fervent charity, and a character of being clothed with humility.

These human accolades truly define the child of God; don't forget to love one another!

Jesus often visited the home of Lazarus and his sisters, Mary and Martha. When he would come to their home, Mary would always sit and listen to his words, while Martha was too busy doing other things. She even complained to Jesus that her sister did not care to help her around the house.

Jesus told Martha that she was too busy and concerned about the little things and that Mary, on the other hand, had chosen the good things, which were to sit at his feet and hear the word. Mary had chosen the principal thing and the most urgent matters (Luke 10:38–42). He realized that Martha's job of cleaning and cooking was very important, but it was even more important to listen and be attentive to the words of the Lord, especially when he was right there in their midst.

The Lord said that the judgmental Pharisees had omitted the weightier matters of the law, which were judgment, mercy, and faith: these concerns were most important (Matt. 23:23). The Lord was trying to tell Martha and the Pharisees that it's only the principle that matters. What is the Lord trying to say? What is he trying to tell us is most important? Mercy, love, judgment, and faith. Martha was concerned about many things, but Mary had chosen the good part!

We are so worried and consumed about so many meaningless things that have absolutely no bearing on our salvation. Maybe we're too focused on how someone else is living to see the bigger picture. We should only be about our Father's business, which is living a godly life and sharing the gospel of Jesus Christ with a lost world.

Let's love one another, for love is the fulfilling of the law (Rom. 13:10). Love works no ill towards his neighbor, for love is of God. Do mediocre actions and minute behaviors in others destroy everything about you? (Really!)

Jesus said to love your neighbor as yourself (Matt. 22:39). As you love yourself, practice loving others the same way. As you forgive yourself for certain deeds done in your body that might not necessarily, please God, then forgive others of their trespasses. Your forgiveness of others is not a license for them to sin, but an indication of the spirit of mercy within you that might win them to Christ.

Just be a light. Let your focus be on living holy yourself. Be the light of the world; a city that's set on a hill that cannot be hidden. Don't be deranged about what others are doing. Just make sure that you're not doing these same things yourself. In short, leave people alone! Be a light in darkness!

Please allow God to rule and judge the world. He really doesn't need any of our help in determining who's saved or where mankind will spend eternity. If he decides to show grace and mercy to whomever, then he can; after all, he's God and he doesn't have to get our permission to bless others. The Lord told Moses that he would have mercy on whomever he decides to, and he would render compassion on whomever he desires to render compassion. In other words, because he's God, he does whatever he wants.

Some tend to wonder whether God is fair in pardoning some for their many transgressions. Romans 9:20–21 reads:

> Nay but, O man, who art thou that replies against God? Shall the thing formed say to him that formed it, why hast thou made me thus? Hath not the potter power over the clay, of the same lump to make one vessel unto honor, and another unto dishonor?

Remember, God is in control. He does whatever he wants to and could care less about how we feel about the way he does it.

Paul continues his admonitions to the church at Rome. Romans 11:33–34 reads, "O the depth of the riches of the wisdom and knowledge of God! how unsearchable are his judgements, and his ways past finding out! For whom hath known the mind of the Lord? or who hath been his counsellor?" The last time I checked, the Lord was still on the throne, still in control, and still running things. Who knows the mind of God? Please stay out of his business. You do your job, witness and make disciples, and let God do his.

Let's learn to minister in our own lane. Peter was the apostle to the Jews; Paul was the apostle to the Gentiles. Both were servants of our Lord. They both had a mission to win souls for the kingdom of Christ, whether Jew or Gentile, for both Jew and Gentile needed a real relationship with God. Even in mere disagreements, they worked together, focusing on the greater mission, winning souls.

We are expected to agree as to our purpose, and that is to bring men, women, boys and girls to Christ by whatever means possible. However, that they come to Christ is really all that matters. As Jesus said in Matthew 9:37, "The harvest truly is plenteous, but the laborers are few." Let's all pray that God will send laborers into his harvest. Remember, God needs laborers, not brawlers!

If we as disciples want to do something profitable, then go preach that those men should repent (Mark 6:12), and let's do it with the grace of God. We should all have the heart of God, not willing that any should perish, but that all come to repentance (2 Pet. 2:9).

It would be very beneficial to allow our will to be defeated and God's will to prevail. It's not about us. It's only about the Lord. Paul told the Corinthian church that he desired to know only one thing among them, which was Jesus Christ and him being crucified (1 Cor. 2:2). He focused on his mission, which was introducing Jesus Christ to a dying world, and not his own self-proclaimed glory. He wanted men to be saved.

Remember, he who wins souls is wise. Let's try to initiate positive things when sharing the gospel message. Why not try telling your testimony of how God saved a wretch like you, before you began ministering with the word. I'm convinced that telling your own personal testimony can be very powerful and effective. Please witness with love and kindness first (Rev. 12:11).

Impress God, not man. Stop looking in another's window, trying to expose their every little sin. Share the gospel message; go and tell John your testimony. Wives, stop witnessing with the Bible under your arm, witness with your life!

Your husband is not going to change by your preaching to him 24/7. He will only be converted by what he can see, hear, and observe, and that is a chaste and holy lifestyle, coupled with the fear of God. Don't just talk the talk; we all need to walk the walk (1 Pet. 3:1–4).

Husbands, how can you demand that other men love their wives when your wife has a black eye. (Really!) One could easily say, I can't hear what you're saying because of seeing what you're doing. Just take care of how you live your life before the Lord; be totally responsible for your own personal actions.

I admonish each one of you to sanctify the Lord your God in your hearts, and always be ready to give an answer to every man who asks you the reasons for the hope that lies in you, with fear and trembling (1 Pet. 3:15). Don't be a busybody, always determined to stir up trouble in others' lives. Remember, one who does not offend with their words is considered a perfect individual and able to bridle the whole body (James 3:2).

Just be a witness to the amazing grace that God has shed upon your life. Expound with great joy the life-changing power of an encounter with a loving Savior. If you won't tell it, then someone else will, for the Lord will never leave himself without a witness (Acts 14:17). Be excited to declare to others all the eternal benefits of being saved.

In the future, before offending and judging others, ask yourself these simple and curious questions:

Am I perfect in God's sight?
Have I considered the poor?
Am I kind and compassionate to all?
Is God first in my life?

Am I a true light to a dying world?
Do I have a good name?
When was the last time I sinned?
How do I treat my wife/husband?
Who am I praying for?
If others could testify about me, what would they say?
When was the last time I visited (fellowshipped) with another church denomination?
Has God been merciful to me?
Do I think that God knows what he's doing?
Does God need any of my help to determine who will inherit eternal life?
Did the Lord Jesus shed his blood for all to have a right to the tree of life?
Do I know when others pray a prayer of repentance?
When did God die and leave me in charge?
In our efforts to try to please God, please try to follow these instructions:
Love what God loves; hate what God hates.
Try to drive the wagon down the middle of the road.
Call all right, right; and call all wrong, wrong.
Denounce all sin; praise all righteousness.
Try to get along with all people, especially enemies.
Forgive others their trespasses against you and against God.

I heard that a man told another person that he would be a Christian except for the Christians he knew! Another proclaimed, "I like your Christ, but not his Christians." (How sad!) It troubles me that we can send missionaries across the world to convert sinners, but when these converts come to our country, they are not welcomed, even in our churches. Oh, people of God, let not these things be once named among you, as becometh saints (Eph. 5:3).

Enoch pleased God with his life. He walked perfectly and peacefully with God for three hundred years. One day his friends looked for him and could not find him, for he was "gone." He did not taste death: God simply took him. God gave this powerful testimony that Enoch pleased God! ([Gen. 5:21–24], [Heb. 11:5]).

Contentions and heresies (group, cliques, denominations) are works of the flesh and devastatingly cruel and carnal (Gal. 5:19–21). Foolishness! I say again, we may not all be under the same roof or in the same neighborhood, but we should all love one another while serving the same God. Password to heaven: Love! Love! Love! (Get it)

Ask yourself, what does God think about it?

How does he really feel about certain issues?

In not justifying any, the psalmist stated, "he remembers that they were but flesh" (Ps. 78:39). He has not dealt with us after our sins, nor rewarded us according to our iniquities. As the heavens are high above the earth, so great is his mercy toward them that fear him, for he knows our frame and he remember that we are dust (Ps. 103:10–11, 14). Please consider this: If the Lord should mark iniquities, then who would be able to stand (Ps. 130:3)? We would all do good by saying to the Lord, "Search me, O God, and know my heart: try me, and know my thoughts: And see if there be any wicked way in me and lead me in the way everlasting (Ps. 139:23–24)."

Think about it!

Is it really that serious?

Does that really matter?

Is it really that big of a deal?

Really? C'mon, man!

Remember, it's only the principles that matter!

CHAPTER 9

GOD IS SOVEREIGN

The world should know that the Lord whose name alone is Jehovah is the highest God over all the earth. In the beginning, God said, let there be light and there was light. Through his omnipotent power, he spoke everything into existence.

The Lord is the Sovereign God. He has done whatever that has pleased him in all the earth (Ps. 135:6). He does whatever his soul desires. He is the only wise God; for by his wisdom, he has founded the world and all its inhabitants. He is greatly to be feared above all others.

Who can we compare to our great God? There is no other God besides the Lord. Isaiah recorded these words in Isaiah 44:6: "Thus saith the Lord the King of Israel, and his redeemer the Lord of hosts; I am the first, and I am the last; and beside me there is no God."

He is Alpha and Omega, the beginning and the end. He has no beginning, and his years shall have no end, for in the beginning, God! Even from everlasting to everlasting, Lord, you are God (Ps. 90:1

He is the all-knowing God (Job 28:10,12–13, 20–24), the Omniscient God who even knows the secrets of the heart ([Ps. 44:21], [Ps. 94:11], [John 21:17]). We should marvel and be in awe at his unimaginable knowledge, power, and wisdom. How great is our God!

Man in all his wisdom is vanity, for the foolishness of God is wiser than man. We should acknowledge him in all our ways, and he will direct our paths. If anyone desires wisdom, then let them ask God for wisdom; they should fear the Lord, for the fear of God is the beginning of wisdom.

In trying to comprehend his magnificence and splendor, we must adhere to the fact that God can do anything that he wants to, and that there is nothing that's too hard for him to do ([Gen. 18:14], [Jer. 32:17, 26–27]). All power belongs to our God.

We, as mere mortals, should stop trying to figure out the Almighty God. Paul baffled the Roman church in asking them these questions concerning the Lord. He asked, "For who has known the mind of God? or who has been his counselor? (Rom. 11:34)"

He goes on to say in verse 33, "O the depths of the riches both of the wisdom and knowledge of God! how unsearchable are his judgments, and his ways past finding out!" For of him and through him and to him are all things: to whom be glory forever. Paul understood that there is no finite being who could understand the mysterious ways of Almighty God.

Isaiah 55:8–9 reads, "For my thoughts are not your thoughts, neither are your ways my ways, saith the Lord. For as the heavens are higher than the earth, so are my ways higher than your ways, and my thoughts than your thoughts." We cannot comprehend his ways! God does not think like mortal human beings, nor are his actions comparable in any way to our limited and frivolous character traits. He is at incredible lengths, higher in wisdom and understanding than the wisest of any created being. He is beyond comprehension! His immanence is still almighty! When we think that we've got God figured out over here, he will burst out over there. I ask, who knows the mind of God? Just give up and accept the fact that whatever God does is right and just and is really none of our business! (Selah.)

We can vainly try, but there is no wisdom nor counsel against God. (Proverbs 21:30) Remember, the Lord is still on the throne and in control. He could literally care less about what we think or how we feel about the way he does things. For whom is the Lord mindful of? Please consider this: so far, the world is still going on. The sun still rises and sets where and when it's supposed to. The last time I checked, God was still running things. (Selah.)

Some may be as Israel was and say that the Lord is not fair (Ezek. 33:17). Regardless of what others might say, the Lord is just and truly fair above all others. We that love the Lord know that the Lord is righteous and that there is no iniquity found in our holy God (Job 34:10–12). The Lord is good to all. He has no pleasure in the death of the wicked. His true desire is that all repent and be converted so that they might be saved.

The Sovereign God told Moses in Deuteronomy 32: "See now that I, even I, am he, and there is no god with me: I kill, and I make alive; I wound, and I heal: neither is there any that can deliver out of my hand." He would, repeatedly say to Moses, in the Old Testament, "I am the Lord!"

Hanna reiterated these words in 1 Samuel 2:2–3, 6–7:

> There is none holy as the Lord: for there is none beside thee: neither is there any rock like our God. Talk no more so exceedingly proudly; let not arrogancy come out of your mouth: for the Lord is a God of knowledge, and by him actions are weighed. ... The Lord kills and makes alive: he bringeth down to the grave, and bringeth up. The Lord makes poor, and makes rich: he bringeth low, and lifted.

Both Moses and Hanna realized that the sovereign God is Lord over the entire earth and governs according to his own good pleasure. The Lord God so loved the world that he gave his only begotten Son, that whosoever believes in him should not perish, but have everlasting life. The Lord did not send his son into the world to condemn the world, but that the world through him might be saved (John 3:16–17). He loves his creation.

Jesus did not come to condemn us in our sins, but rather to save us from our sins. God is truly a merciful Savior. How can God show mercy on the vilest of sinners? Is there unrighteousness with God? The answer is no, but God will have mercy on whom he will have mercy and will have compassion on whom he will have compassion (Rom. 9:14–15).

Jesus responded angrily to the self-righteous Pharisees' question in Matthew 9:11–13. When the Pharisees saw it, they said to his disciples, why does your master eat with tax collectors and sinners? But when Jesus heard that, he said to them, "Those that be whole need not need a physician, but they that are sick. But go and learn ye what that meant. I will have mercy, and not sacrifice for I am not come to call the righteous, but sinners to repentance." We should desire the mercy and compassion of the Lord.

Luke Chapter 23 tells us that the thief on the cross hanging next to Jesus asked the Lord to remember him when he came into his glory. Jesus replied, "Today thou shall be with me in Paradice." (Luke 23:43) I'm sure that the dreaded Pharisees would argue that the thief had no right to eternal life; after all, he is a thief and deserves his punishment, for that's why he's on the cross.

Here's the point I'm trying to get across to my readers. Being God, and God alone, the Lord had every right to forgive whomever he wanted to; if he decided to forgive this man, then who in the world could dare question his decision. The Lord forgave him because he knew his heart (Acts 1:24). He said to the thief on the cross, this day you shall be with me in paradise, and he didn't ask for my opinion or approval! (Selah.)

Remember, he is the sovereign God. He's just too wise to make a mistake. His will shall prevail. No matter who fights against it, in the end, God wins! The best and wisest thing for all humanity to do, seriously, is to stay out of his business and be determined not to make him angry. Woe unto the world when God is angry:

it's a fearful thing to fall into the hands of the living God (Heb. 10:31).

Too many are engulfed in the law. I was part of the local church for nearly twenty years. I knew the law like the back of my hand. Yes, I knew the law, but I had no clue about grace. I didn't realize that the law was given by Moses, but grace and truth came by Jesus Christ (John 1:17). I failed to realize that the greatest thing about grace is it's amazing! People today need grace, not condemnation!

That thief on the cross called him Lord. He had faith in who Jesus was. He knew that Jesus was the Son of God, the Lord from heaven. The thief knew that there was life after death. Jesus said, this day you shall be with me in paradise. The Lord counted this man's faith for righteousness, as he did Abraham's and yours and mine. Jesus said in John 11:25–26, "He that believeth in me, though he were dead, yet shall he live: And whosoever who lives and believeth in me shall never die."

Regardless of what the Pharisees or any others have to say, that thief is in heaven with the Lord and no longer a thief. He is forgiven because God knew his heart, and God can exact forgiveness on whomever he pleases. Yes, he's no longer a thief because of an understanding and merciful God.

I don't know who God will allow into heaven, for it's really none of my business. If the Lord allows me into eternal life, then whoever else he allows in is fine and dandy. Again, I'm not God. He's in charge. I'll stay out of it, for its none of my business. He doesn't need my help to determine who's saved and who's not. If the Lord would allow me, I'll just be "light" and stay out of his way and allow him to be "judge."

No one will go to heaven that's not supposed to go, no one! But that's not my call. He's got this. The Lord is just too wise to make a mistake. He has the last say. He really knows what he is doing. Baffled? God was judging the world before I was born; when I'm dead and gone, he will still be judging the world and doing a good job of it.

And if you're wondering, no one will slip through the back door or climb over the fence into heaven. Jesus said in John 10:7, "Verily, verily, I say unto you, I am the door of the sheep." John 10:9 reads, "I am the door: by me if any man enters in, he shall be saved, and shall go in and out, and find pasture." He concludes in John 14:6 by saying, "I am the way, the truth and the life: no man cometh unto the Father, but by me." The Lord will determine who inherits eternal life!

I'm so glad that man won't determine where we spend eternity. If things were left up to man, then man would be just who he is: man. Thankfully, God, the righteous judge, will oversee all judgment according to his holy providence, sovereignty, and omnipotent wisdom. God's got this! Hallelujah!

The Lord is not as interested in rituals and sacrifices as he is in a truly repented heart. Just be real. Repent yourself of your sins. Strive to be holy every day you live upon the face of the earth. All throughout his holy word, God reminds us of his mercy. Please remember that the Lord is good, his mercy is everlasting, and his truth endures to all generations. He is certainly justified and in authority to forgive whomever he pleases.

I'm convinced that if one would truly repent, express Godly sorrow, and ask God to forgive him of his sins, the Almighty God, being merciful, will forgive his most egregious sins, remove them far from him, and remember them no more. It's a done deal, for it's the very nature of God. It's just who he is.

Because he's the sovereign Lord, he knows what he's doing. It is because of the Lord's mercy that we are not consumed in his anger. We can't function on our own, for by him, we move and breathe and have our being. Please trust the sovereign God to be who he has always been, the Lord of glory! O sovereign God, please keep being who you are!

The prophet sums it all up in Isaiah 45:5–7:

I am the Lord, and there is none else, there is no God

beside me: I girded thee, though thou hast not known me: That they may know from the rising of the sun, and from the west, that there is none beside me. I am the Lord, and there is no one else. I form the light, and create darkness: I make peace, and create evil: I the Lord do all these things.

To the sovereign God, be glory and majesty forever, amen!

CHAPTER 10

BACK TO EDEN

In the garden of Eden, God had fellowship with his creation. The God of Heaven and Earth came down and tabernacled with Adam and Eve. He enjoyed his intimate relationship with them. There was a perfect environment and relationship between God and his creation, until sin entered the garden.

The sin of disobedience separated mankind from God. Man's sin ruined a perfect relationship with God and caused the curse of sorrow, disease, and death to infiltrate a perfect world. God cast the man and his wife out of the garden, thus severing our much-needed relationship with him.

But thankfully, God had a plan to reconcile mankind back to himself. The Bible tells us that Jesus Christ was slain in the mind of God before the foundation of the world ([1 Pet. 1:20], [Rev. 13:8]).

God knows the end before the beginning (Isa. 46:9–10). To put it in terminology that everyone can understand, before God created man, he knew that man would fall. Therefore, God had a plan to restore mankind unto himself even before he created him. The untainted precious blood of our Lord Jesus Christ was shed as the propitiation for our sins.

Yes, before man sinned, God had a remedy for his sins: the shed blood of his only begotten son. Jesus Christ, the Son of God, did appease the anger of Almighty God. He was the ransom and satisfaction to acquire God's mercy and forgiveness. He became sin for us. He was the emotional battering ram; Calvary's cross took sin's death sentence away (2 Cor. 5:21).

Isaiah 53:10–12 reads:

> Yet it pleased the Lord to bruise him; he has put him to grief: when thou shalt make his soul an offering for sin, he shall see his seed, he shall prolong his days, and the pleasure of the Lord shall prosper in his hand. He shall see the travail of his soul and shall be satisfied: by his knowledge shall my righteous servant justify many; for he shall bear their iniquities. Therefore, will I divide him a portion with the great, and he shall divide the spoil with the strong; because he hath poured out his soul unto death: and he was numbered with the transgressors; and bare the sins of many, and made intercession for the transgressors.

For God so loved, he gave! Jesus made it possible for us to have a renewed relationship with God, for he reconciled us through his blood! People truly need a relationship with God. The world needs a savior. Men have many things, but they are not satisfied, for they have no savior. The inhabitants of this world lack an intimate relationship with the Lord.

Have you ever wondered, if you died today, where you would spend eternity? If the Lord came today, would you go back with him? Are you watching and waiting for the immanent return of the Lord? I seriously admonish you to be always ready, for we don't know the day or the hour that our Lord is coming. It would be wise and very beneficial to surrender your life unto the Lord today. Please don't wait for tomorrow, for tomorrow is not promised to any of us. Therefore, as a child of God, endure the pain and despise the shame in living a persecuted-yet-saved life, for it will all be worth it after a while.

Jesus is coming again soon! As the disciples watched the Lord ascend into the clouds toward the heavens, the angels assured them that he would come again just as he had gone away. That's the hope of the saints, for we look for that blessed hope and the glorious appearing of the great God and our Savior, Jesus Christ. Our attitude should be please come, Lord Jesus.

For those that look for him, he shall appear the second time without sin unto salvation (Heb. 9:28). Keep your lamps burning and your lights shining bright, for at midnight a cry will be made: Behold the bridegroom comes, let's all go out to meet him. For it's the midnight cry, and then we'll be going home!

Deuteronomy 33:1–3 reads:

> And this is the blessing, wherewith Moses the man of God blessed the children of Israel before his death. And he said, The Lord came from Sinai, and rose from Seir unto them; he shined forth from mount Peran, and he came with ten thousand of saints: from his right hand went a fiery law for them. Yea, he loved the people; all his saints are in thy hand: and they sat down at thy feet; everyone shall receive of thy words.

The same sentiments are echoed in Jude 14: "And Enoch also, the seventh from Adam, prophesied of these, saying, 'Behold, the Lord cometh with ten thousand of his saints.'" Both Moses and Enoch saw the Lord of Glory coming with his saints. I've also seen an innumerable number of believers coming with the Lord to enjoy heaven on earth.

When the Lord returns, he will miraculously and powerfully change the whole atmosphere here on earth. We will return to the days as it was in the garden of Eden. Jesus told his disciples "I go away to prepare a place for you; if I go and prepare a place for you, then I will return and receive you unto myself, that wherever I am, there you may be also." (John 14:1-4)

The Lord will gather all the saints as one unto him. The meek shall inherit the earth. During the millennial age, the thousand-year reign of the Lord here on the earth, we the people of God shall enjoy a Utopian atmosphere with him. Yes, when the Lord returns, he will redeem mankind to a renewed and righteous relationship with him. Praise God!

In this millennium, God shall restore the earth to its former state. The curse placed on the earth and mankind shall be removed. The Lord will reign from the Holy City, the new Jerusalem. He will be the long-awaited King of kings and Lord of Lords. There will truly be peace on earth and good will toward all men; for the Prince of Peace will be among us. (Glory!)

Some have many things but are not happy, for possessions don't make us happy. They covet things that will one day perish. We brought nothing into this world, and it is certain that we will carry nothing out. The word of God tells us that happy are those whose God is the Lord. The Lord's presence, a real relationship with him, the absence of sin, and the banishing of the devil from the earth will bring true happiness.

Be content and satisfied with what you have here on this earth. You may not receive it in this present world but rejoice that your names are written in heaven. It's not about this side, but the life to come (the other shore). God will faithfully provide everything that we need. The Lord will give us life and that, more abundantly.

The patriarch Abraham looked for a city whose builder and maker is God. He and so many others all died, not having received the promises of God. Having seen them afar off and being persuaded of them, they embraced them and confessed that they were strangers and pilgrims on the earth (Heb. 11:13).

In Eden, there will be a pure river of life proceeding out of the throne of God and of the lamb. Amid the street on both sides of the river is the tree of life, which shall bear twelve manners of fruits, whose leaves are for the healing of nations.

When we return to Eden, God shall create a new atmosphere,

where there shall be a new heaven and a new earth and all the former things shall be remembered no more, nor come to mind. The Lord shall rejoice in his people, and the voice of weeping shall never be heard again. There will be no more an infant of days, neither shall there be an old man that has not fulfilled his days. A thousand years shall be as one day, and one day shall be as a thousand years.

Men shall build houses and inhabit them, and they shall plant vineyards and eat the fruit thereof. We shall live forever, for as the tree is, so shall be the life of God's people on the earth. God's elect shall forever enjoy the work of their hands. Because we are the seed of the highest, we shall glory in his splendor and be amazed because of the abundance of his riches. When we are in need, before we call, he will answer; and while we are still speaking, he will hear. The wolf and the lamb shall feed together. The lion shall eat straw like the cattle, and the dust shall be the serpent's meat. None shall hurt or destroy in all of God's holy mountains (Isa. 65:17–25).

All warriors will turn their swords into plowshares, and they will study war no more (Micah 4:3). If you're wondering when the kingdom of God will come, well, I'll let you know that the kingdom of God is already here, for the kingdom of God is in you (Luke 17:20–22). We wait for the coming of our King from heaven, the Lord Jesus, the Christ. He will reign forever from the new Jerusalem, the City of God prepared by God for his bride, the church.

God has prepared a beautiful place for a prepared people. If you've been risen with Christ, seek those things which are above, where Christ sits on the right hand of God. Wherefore, set your affections on things above and not on things of this earth. For we all who love him are dead, and our lives are hidden with Christ in God. Therefore, when Christ, who is our life, shall appear, then we shall appear with him in glory (Col. 3:1–3).

I show you all a mystery: not all of us shall sleep, because some of us, the body of Christ, shall be changed in a moment, in the twinkling of an eye. Loved ones and friends will ask, has anybody seen my old friend Larry?

One of these mornings, and it won't be long, you're going to look for me and I'll be gone-gone-gone. Please keep watching, therefore, for you know not the day when the Lord shall call his church away. If you're striving, striving for the right, you shall wear a golden crown; for when my journey's over, I'll be going home!

Be encouraged Saints; for our light afflictions, which are just for a moment, work for us a far more exceeding and eternal weight of glory (2 Cor. 4:17). Therefore, I reckon that the sufferings of this present time are not worthy to be compared to the glory that shall be revealed in us (Rom. 8:18). Jesus is coming to set up his kingdom here on earth.

From the very beginning, before he even spoke creation into existence, God had a plan. His ultimate desire was to tabernacle with his creation. John said in Revelation 21:3, "And I heard a great voice out of heaven saying, Behold, the tabernacle of God is with men, and he will dwell with them, and they shall be his people, and God himself shall be with them, and be their God." Goodbye, old world, goodbye!

Oh, what a glorious time when we return to Eden. Praise God!

SUMMARY

John the Baptist came preaching "Repent, for the kingdom of Heaven is at hand" (Matt. 3:2). The Lord Jesus said, "Except ye repent, ye'll likewise perish" (Luke 13:3). Paul made it very clear to the Gentiles in Thessalonica that in times past God winked at these sins, but now commands all men everywhere to repent (Acts 17:30).

God's plan of salvation is simple to understand, if one seeks God's guidance and his divine clarity. Romans 10:9–10 reads, "if you shalt confess with thy mouth the Lord Jesus and shall believe in thine heart that God hath raised him from the dead, thou shalt be saved. For with the heart man believeth unto righteousness; and with the mouth confession is made unto salvation."

This same Bible states in Acts 2:36–38: "Therefore let all the house of Israel know assuredly, that God hath made that same Jesus, whom ye have crucified, both Lord and Christ. Now when they heard this, they were pricked in their heart, and said unto Peter and to the rest of the apostles, Men and brethren, what shall we do? Then Peter said unto them, Repent, and be baptized every one of you in the name of Jesus Christ for the remission of sins, and ye shall receive the gift of the Holy Ghost."

His holy dialogue continues in Acts 3:19: "Repent ye therefore, and be converted, that your sins may be blotted out, when the times of refreshing shall come from the presence of the Lord."

These words are recorded in John 3:5: "Jesus answered, Verily, verily, I say unto thee, except a man be born of water and of the Spirit, he cannot enter into the kingdom of God." The Lord's words continue in John 3:36: "He that believeth on the Son hath everlasting life: and he that believeth not on the Son shall not see life; but the wrath of God abides on him." Repentance starts the salvation process and restores our relationship with Christ. True repentance allows us to approach him.

It's quite simple, and even the lowest novice should be able to perceive what the word is saying. Sadly, however, not all have this knowledge. Luke 24:45 reads, "Then opened he their understanding, that they might understand the scriptures." Sadly, too many students are too stubborn, and will not allow the master teacher, the Lord, to open their understanding. These so-called know-it-alls will never get it.

Some truly believe that their denomination or beliefs are the only right way to heaven. If one is looking to find their side of heaven, then they will find it. Those desiring to go to a segregated, separated, and isolated heaven will surely get there; unfortunately, it's called the lake that burns with fire, and you don't want to go there!

All of us that are fortunate and blessed to inherit eternal life will all go to the same place and serve the same God. There's no white side, black side, your church side, nor my church side: for there's only one side (you guessed it), God's side!

Leave people alone; live holy; share the Gospel message; be an effective witness; just be light; pray for others; seek God's guidance as to how to interact with other people. Love truly defines us. Love for God and our fellowman tells the world that we belong to the Lord, for without God's love, we have no witnessing power. It's simple: love God and love your fellow man. Be determined not to put a stumbling block in another's path to cause them to fall. If we do these things, we'll please our Lord.

I heard a man say, "When the saints go to heaven, they will be surprised at who will be in heaven, and even more surprised as to who won't be there." (Wow!) I have, however, concluded that what the Lord really wants us to do is to love him with all our mind, our soul, and all our strength; and to show the Lord that we love him by loving others as we love ourselves. That's the greatest of commandments (Matt. 22:34–40).

We should all have one common goal: to make it to heaven.

We should all have one common desire: to please God.

We should all be driven by the same determined purpose: to share the gospel message.

We should be insanely fueled to be a light to a dying world.

Our love for God should be accompanied by a serious desire to love one another.

We should be possessed by a fervent and blessed hope to see Jesus.

We need to be inspired by a heavenly vision to witness the gathering of the church (the body of Christ and the saints).

We all shall be changed in a moment, in the twinkling of an eye.

We should be engulfed with a passionate longing for the coming of our Lord and Savior, Jesus Christ. Revelation 22:20 reads, "He which testifies these things saith, surely I come quickly." Amen. Even so, come Lord Jesus.

Is Christ divided? Certainly not, and neither should we be divided!

Jesus said that a house divided against itself cannot stand. I'm not your enemy, and you are certainly not mine. We're all in this thing together. We've all got a home in that land, as brothers and sisters in Christ.

If we all work together, as the body of Christ, we'll accomplish our goal and receive a glorious and heavenly crown and reward from our Lord and Savior, Jesus Christ. When we all get to heaven, what a day of rejoicing there will be. When we all see Jesus, we will sing and shout the victory.

Why can't we love one another and treat one another in a way that pleases God? Why all the division and fussing and fighting? Why can't we, as brothers and sisters, love one another as Christ loves us?

Living, loving, sharing, caring.

Get right, church, and let's go home.

God bless you, in Jesus's name!

Is Christ divided? (Selah.)

ABOUT THE AUTHOR

Elder Larry Young is a Pentecostal preacher and proclaimer of the gospel of Jesus Christ. He considers himself a very rare and unique individual. He says that he credits a lot of his character and demeanor to his childhood upbringing, namely precise rearing and raising by his mother and father.

He accounts his early years of life and that being raised in a black-and-white neighborhood instilled in him a sense of determination to try to be a vivid peacemaker and get along with everybody in order that life would be so much better and very rewarding.

He found out early in life that one could catch more flies with honey than with vinegar. With his parents reminding him to be nice, tolerant, and kind, many doors were opened for him that would normally be closed in his face. An eagerness to get along with others, regardless of race or social status, began to literally shape his life well before accepting his call to the ministry.

Having received his calling at fifteen years old but not fully accepting or understanding that calling until age thirty-five, Elder Larry Young found himself in a situation of having a way to go in fulfilling God's call on his life, predestined mission, and divine purpose. He believes that there is a great zeal within him to unite the body of Christ and get past racial and denominational foolishness and basically say to all of us who love the Lord, "Why can't we get along?"

Even in his early high school years, he crossed racial and cultural lines to be friends with others of different ethnic backgrounds. It didn't seem to bother him what neighborhood you came from or whether you attended a church of a particular denomination. He just wanted to be friends.

Now this Pentecostal preacher, with God's guidance and direction, finds himself breaking down racial and denominational barriers and differences by visiting and fellowshipping with all whom God sends him to congregate and associate with. He strongly believes that all who walk upright and please God with their lives by loving one another will go to the same place, which is God's glorious heaven, prepared for the saints of God! Praise God!

Elder Larry Young tells all who will listen that there is one God, one heaven, one people. If you can't get along down here, love one another, and treat one another in a way that pleases Almighty God, then there is no need in looking to go to God's prepared heavenly kingdom. Larry Young says, "Every time I cross paths with someone who may not seem to like me for whatever reason, my assignment becomes to win that person to Christ by whatever means possible." Souls: that's all that really matters!

Like the apostle Paul, Elder Young is asking all who are engaged in division, separation, isolation, segregation, and non-association this question: "Is Christ divided?" I mean, really! A divided, segregated heaven? C'mon, man! Why can't we, as God's people, love one another and get along?